Włodzimierz Rędzioch

FATIMA
AND
SURROUNDINGS

Distributed by:
DAVID DA SILVA

Magagia Sta Catarina da Serra
tel. 044/741375
2495 FATIMA

Published and printed by

NARNI - TERNI

Fatima - a Portuguese village

On a map of the Iberian Peninsula today we see two independent countries, Portugal and Spain.

However, in the past, the destinies of these two countries were closely linked. Under Augustus the peninsula was divided into three provinces: Lusitania, Betica and Terraconensis.

The west coast belonged to the province of Lusitania whose capital was Merida. Later these lands were invaded by the Svevi (416-584) and the Visigoths (584-712). Arab occupation began in the 8th century and lasted for more than three centuries. This time the invaders came from the South. In 711, Arab troops led by Tarik crossed the Strait of Gibraltar and began the Muslim conquest of the peninsula. On the territory of present day Portugal and Spain, the Arabs founded an important caliphate.

Teeming with life, it was not only a commercial but an artistic and cultural centre. In the 12th century, the northern part of Portugal was already in Christian hands, while the lands south of the River Tagus still formed part of the Caliphate. A legend from this period explains how the village of Fatima got its name.

On the 24th June 1158, a group of ladies-in-waiting and Arab knights left Alcacer do Sal Castle to picnic on the banks of the River Sado. Unexpectedly, the procession was attacked by a group of armed Christians led by Gonçalo Hermingues known as the "Mooriighter". In a brief battle, the Arabs were overwhelmed and brought to Santarém, the city where Afonso Henriques, the first Portuguese monarch, resided.

The king wished to reward the valiant knight and asked him what he desired most. Gonçalo asked for the hand of Fatima, the most beautiful and noble of the captured damsels. Afonso Henriques promised to give his consent to the marriage on two conditions, that Fatima herself agreed, and that she became a Christian.

The young woman, obviously already in love with the handsome knight, consented and became a Christian, taking the name of Oureana. The young couple received the village of Abdegas as a wedding present. Gonçalo changed the name of the place to Oureana (nowadays Ourém).

Unfortunately, the beautiful Oureana died young. Her distraught husband sought consolation in the Monastery of St. Bernard in Alcobáça, 30 km to the west of Oureana. A few years later, the abbot had the body of Gonçalo' s wife brought to a small

church built nearby. From that moment on, the place became known as Fatima. Divine Providence willed that the city of Our Lady bore the name of a daughter of Mohammed.

In the centuries that followed, Fatima was not mentioned in the chronicles. It was too small even to appear on a map. Life in the village was peaceful, following the pattern of the seasons and the working of the fields. At the beginning of the century, the population in the village and its outlying hamlets was around 2,000 and the inhabitants earned their living from agriculture, particularly sheep farming, and spinning and weaving.

Although only 130 km from the capital, Fatima was unaffected by the great events troubling Portugal, the great recession, the First World War, parliamentary in-fighting and the government's anti-clerical policies.

As early as 1911, the Prime Minister, Afonso Costa, introduced a law separating the Church from the State. With this, the authorities hoped to "liquidate" the Catholic religion in the space of two generations.

The government pursued a policy of repression of the clergy and the press incited the people against the Church.

Often students were compelled to participate in anti-clerical demonstrations and carry banners with slogans such as "Neither God nor religion!" The absence of means of communication in the countryside led to the "blessed" isolation of the small, self-sufficient villages and the simple people who lived there.

The year 1917 was a crucial one in the history of Fatima - an unknown village in the Estremadura hills became the stage for one of the most important religious events of the 20th century - the apparitions of Our Lady.

The little shepherds of Aljustrel

Aljustrel is a small hamlet lying to the west of Fatima. There, among others, lived two inter-related families - the dos Santos and the Marto. On 22nd March 1907, Maria Rosa dos Santos gave birth to her seventh and last child, a girl, baptised Lucia in the local parish church. On the 11th March of the following year, Olimpia and Manuel Pedro Marto celebrated the birth of their son Francisco (Olimpia and Lucia's father were sister and brother, thus Lucia and Francisco were cousins). On the 10th March 1910 a girl, Jacinta, was also born into the Marto family. Many years later, in her letters to the Bishop of Leiria, Lucia described her happy childhood in touching detail.[*] Lucia, being the youngest, was particularly doted upon by her unmarried sisters who were still at home and by her parents. Her sisters brought her everywhere with them and little Lucia was always present at the dances and simple diversions of the youth of the village. And there was always an excuse for a dance - the grape-harvest, the gathering of the olives, harvest and every religious festival usually ended with a lucky dip and a dance, not to mention the wedding banquets which lasted all night. Maria Rosa was greatly respected in the village and was always invited to celebrations and parties. As well as this two of Lucia's sisters worked as dressmakers and were always making dresses for their liIlle sister. They also taught Lucia how to dance. The peaceful atmosphere in the dos Santos home attracted young people from all over the area. They all spent Sunday evenings in front of their house, talking and inventing new games. Maria Rosa taught the children their Catechism. In the summer she taught them during the afternoon siesta and in the winter evenings in front of the open fire where they roasted chestnuts. Lucia learned quickly and at the age of only six, having passed the exam with the parish priest, she was able to receive her First Communion. It was a memorable day for the young girl. The night before Lucia was unable to sleep and spent the night helping her sisters sew her white dress. This is what Sister Lucia writes about the event: "And finally the happy day dawned, but how long it was until 9 o'clock when, with my white dress on, my sister Maria carried me into the kitchen to beg my parents forgiveness, kiss their hands and ask for their blessing. This ceremony over, my mother gave me her last words of advice. She told me what she wanted me to ask Our Lord when he was in my breast and sent me off with these words, 'Above all, ask Our Lord to make you a saint', words that remained so strongly imprinted on my mind that they were the first I said to

4

The three little shepherds chosen by the Virgin: Lucia, Francisco and Jacinta.

Our Lord when I received him. And even today I can still hear the echo of my mother's voice repeating these words to me. I started off with my sisters towards the church. My brother carried me to protect me from the dirt and dust of the road. As soon as I got to the church, I ran to the altar of Our Lady where I renewed my request. There I stayed in contemplation of the smile from the evening before, until my sisters came to bring me to my place. There were many children, forming four rows from the door of the church up to the balustrade, two rows of boys and two of girls. Since I was the smallest, I had the place next to the angels on the balustrade step. The sung Mass began and as the moment gradually drew near, my heart beat faster and faster, awaiting the visit of a great God, coming down from heaven to be united with my poor soul. The reverend Father came down along the rows to distribute the bread of the angels. I had the good fortune to be first. As the priest came down the steps of the altar, my heart felt as if it would burst. But as soon as I felt the Divine Host on my lips I felt a lasting serenity and peace; I was flooded with such a supernatural sensation and the presence of Our Good Lord was so palpable that it was as if I saw him and heard him with my bodily senses. I addressed my supplications to him: 'Lord, make me a saint. Preserve my heart for ever pure, only for You'." Her First Communion

had an enormous impact on the spiritual life of the young girl - even today Sister Lucia speaks of that day as one of the most important moments in her life.

Until 1914, Lucia had no special chores within the family. Her parents and elder sisters worked in the fields, tended the sheep, did the weaving and looked after the house. Very often her mother helped their neighbours to care for the sick. Francisco and Jacinta Marto's childhood was very similar. Francisco was calm and a little reserved. He hated conflict and was easy-going. He enjoyed being alone and played with others only when invited to do so. He played the pipe and sang. He loved animals and always fed the birds. One day he spent all his savings to free a caged bird which had been captured by boys in a nearby village. He also played with

Aljustrel, parish of Fatima (photo from beginning of the century).

lizards and snakes and fed them sheep's milk. Jacinta did not resemble her brother either in looks or character. Sensitive and thoughtful, she was also lively and obstinate while at the same time delicate and kind. She was an excellent dancer and loved animals, playing with the lambs she often brought home on her shoulders, "so they wouldn't get tired" as she used to say. Lucia admits that at the beginning she was not drawn to her cousins. Francisco was too calm, Jacinta too touchy. They, however, always sought Lucia's company, she was full of life and initiative. They played together behind the dos Santos' house near the well or in the farmyard in the shade of the figtrees. Lucia was the first catechist of the cousins and while she was preparing for her First Communion, she told them everything she had learnt about the faith from the parish priest and her mother. Often certain aspects arose which caused them problems. Once Jacinta wanted to participate in the Corpus Christi procession. Her cousin explained to her that she was to throw the flowers at the Lord Jesus carried by the parish priest. During the procession Jacinta never took her eyes off the priest but did not throw even one petal. After the ceremony her cousin asked her: "Jacinta, why did you not throw the flowers at Jesus?" "Because I didn't see him. Did you see Baby Jesus?" "No, but do you not know that Baby Jesus in the Host is invisible? You can't see him, he's hidden. That's what we receive in communion." From that day onwards Jacinta and Francisco called the Host " Hidden Jesus".

Jacinta, Lucia and Francisco.

7

The apparitions of the Angel

In 1915, Lucia's sister, Carolina, reached her thirteenth birthday and could, according to the custom of the time, work in the fields and learn to become a seamstress. Now it was Lucia's turn to tend the family flock of sheep. They normally grazed on the hill known as Cabeço not far from Aljustrel. One day Lucia, who today does not remember the precise date because she was unable to distinguish the months from the years and not even the days of the week, brought the sheep to the southern slope of the hill. She was in the company of other shepherdesses, Teresa Matias, her sister Maria Rosa and Maria Justina from the village of Casa Velha. About midday, after eating their lunch, the girls began to say the rosary. And as they prayed, an extraordinary thing happened. Lucia described it in this way, "We had just begun, when we saw before our eyes a figure, like a statue made of snow. It hung as if suspended in mid-air, above the woods, and seemed almost transparent in the light of the sun's rays. 'What on earth is that?', asked the girls, a little afraid. 'I don't know.' 'We continued our prayers with our eyes fixed on that figure which disappeared as soon as we had finished. I, as was my wont, decided to say nothing to anyone about what I had seen, but my friends, as soon as they arrived home, told their families what had happened. The news

spread. One day I arrived home and my mother asked me. 'Tell me. They say you saw someone up there on the hill. Can you tell me what it was you saw?' 'I don't know', and since I did not know how to explain myself, I added, 'It seemed like a person wrapped in a sheet.' And trying to explain that I had not been able to see the features I said, 'It was impossible to see the eyes or the hands'. 'Children's foolishness', said my mother and ended the conversation with a gesture of scorn. Time passed and we went back with our flocks to the same spot and the same thing happened, in the same way. My friends again told everyone what we had seen. And the same thing happened a third time a short while after. It was the third time that my mother had heard outsiders speaking about these events without me saying anything at all in the house. She called me to her, dissatisfied, and asked me: 'Tell me now, what is it that you see up there.' 'I don't know, Mother, I don't know what it is.' The following year Francisco and Jacinta's parents allowed them to tend their family flock although they were still too young. Lucia gave up the company of the other girls and brought her flock to pasture with her cousins who were so fond of her. Every morning they met at the same time near the small lake known as Barreiro at the foot of the hill. Here they let their flocks run together and decided where to go to graze them. Tending the sheep was not a difficult job so the children had lots of time to play. Their favourite games were flicking stones, forfeits, tiddly winks and cards. They danced and sang and Francisco played his pipe. The children also found time for the rosary and religious songs. In her memoirs, Lucia admits that often, in order to have more time to play, the children devised a way of saying the rosary in a hurry, they said only the words "Hail Mary" on each bead and just the words "Our Father" at the end. This is the way the little shepherds of Aljustrel spent their days. One day, Lucia, Francisco and Jacinta brought their flocks to the field known as the "Chousa Velha" which belonged to the dos Santos family. As it started to rain early in the morning, the children moved towards an olive grove belonging to Lucia's godfather. There were small caves there and there they took shelter. In the afternoon the weather got better but the little shepherds remained in the caves, playing games. A strong wind blew up unexpectedly and shook the trees, and immediately afterwards the children saw a white figure above the olive trees. As they drew near, the little shepherds saw that it was a young boy, very beautiful and white and almost transparent, as if made of crystal. He came towards the astonished children and said: "Do not be afraid. I am the Angel of Peace. Pray with me." Kneeling down and bowing his head low, the heavenly creature prayed: "O God, I believe in You, I adore You, I have hope in You and I love You! I ask You to pardon those who do not adore You, love You or have hope in You." Then he asked them to repeat the prayer three times and rose saying, "Pray this way. The Hearts of Jesus and Mary hear the voice of your supplication." The apparition of the Angel had such an effect on the children that, immersed in prayer, they lost their sense of time. Lucia remembers that they felt the presence of God so strongly that they did not dare speak among themselves. None of them spoke to their parents about their miraculous encounter. It must be mentioned that Francisco could see the Angel but could not hear his words, so he learnt the prayer from the girls. The second apparition of the Angel took place in the summer of the same year (1916). During the afternoon siesta, the children were playing behind the dos Santos house near the well known as Arniero. Suddenly the same white figure appeared saying "What are you doing? You must pray, you must pray incessantly. The Sacred Hearts of Jesus and Mary h ave intentions of mercy for you. You must constantly offer prayers and sacrifices to the Most High." Lucia then asked what sacrifices they should make and received the following reply: "Offer to God every sacrifice you can, as an act of contrition for sins against Him and to beg for the conversion of sinners. In this way you can bring peace to our land. I am your guardian angel, the angel of Portugal. Above all accept and endure in submission the suffering Our Lord will send you." They were all very shaken and no longer had any desire to play or talk. From that moment on, they began to avoid the company of other children of their own age in order to devote themselves completely to prayer and meditation. As had happened in the first vision, Francisco did not hear the words of the Angel, and asked the girls to repeat them to him. The Angel appeared for the third time in September or October. The children were tending their flocks on the mountain above Valinhos. After their midday meal, they decided to go and pray in the cave. Kneeling, they were repeating the Angel's prayer when the white figure appeared again. This time the heavenly messenger held a chalice and a Host. Drops of blood fell from the Host into the chalice. All of a sudden the Angel left the Host and the chalice suspended in mid-air and kneeling, repeated the following prayer three times: "O Most Sacred Trinity, Father, Son and Holy Spirit, I offer up to You the most precious body, blood, soul and divinity of Jesus Christ, present in all the tabernacles of the earth, in atonement for all the outrages, sacrileges and indifference with which He has been offended. And for the infinite goodness of His Sacred Heart and the Immaculate Heart of Mary, I beseech You for the

conversion of poor sinners." Then he rose and gave the chalice to the children saying: "Take and drink the body and blood of Jesus Christ, horribly offended by ungrateful men. Atone for their crimes and console your God." After this miraculous communion the Angel disappeared. The children remained as if paralysed and only at nightfall realised they had to bring home the sheep. The following days were so full of supernatural feeling that they did not dare talk about it. Francisco, remembering the apparitions of the Angel, said: "I really like seeing the Angel, but the bad thing is that afterwards we are unable to do anything! I wasn't even able to walk afterwards. I didn't know what was wrong with me." Despite their physical weakness however, the young shepherds were full of inner peace and joy.

The apparitions of our Lady

In 1917, Lucia was ten, Francisco nine and Jacinta seven. Life went on in the usual way with the young shepherds tending their flocks daily on the hills around Aljustrel. On Sunday 13th May after Holy Mass, all three of them went to the pasture belonging to the dos Santos family known as "Cova da Iria". It was a beautiful spring morning. About midday, the children ate their lunch and began to play, building a small stone wall.

Suddenly they saw something similar to a flash of lightning. Fearing a storm, they decided to return home. On their way down the hillside they saw another flash and immediately afterwards, the figure of a woman appeared, shining bright like the sun, above a holm oak. The lady, dressed in white and suspended in the air, was no more than a metre and a half away from the children who were enveloped in her rays . Between the "lady dressed in white" and Lucia the following dialogue ensued:

"Do not be afraid, I do not want to hurt you."

"Where do you come from?", she asked.

"From heaven."

"And what do you want me to do?"

"I have come to ask you to come here for six months in succession on the 13th of each month at this same time. Then I will tell you who I am and what I want from you. Then I will come back here again a seventh time."

"And will I go to heaven too?"

"Yes, you will."

"And Jacinta?"

"She will too."

"And Francisco?"

"He too, but he will have to say many rosaries.

Do you want to offer yourselves to God and to endure all the suffering He will send you as an act of contrition for the sins of those who have wronged Him and petition Him for the conversion of sinners?"

"Yes, we do."

"Then you will suffer much, but the grace of God will be your comfort."

At that moment, urged by an inner impulse, they fell to their knees and repeated: "O Most Sacred Trinity, I adore You. My God, My God, I adore You in the MQst Sacred Sacrament."

At the end the Lady added: "Say the rosary every day, to bring peace to the world and bring about the end of the war."

It must be mentioned that only Lucia - the oldest of the three children - spoke with Our Lady.

Jacinta could see and hear "the lady", but Francisco could only see Her but heard nothing, like in the visions of the Angel. After the vision of Our Lady, the little shepherds felt full of joy and enthusiasm. Unlike the visions of the angel, the encounter with Mary filled them with energy. All three of them decided to say nothing to anyone about the vision.

However that very evening, Jacinta told her parents everything. Crying, she begged Lucia' s forgiveness and explained that something inside her prevented her from keeping silent. Immediately the news spread through the village. Francisco and Jacinta's parents were understanding but Lucia' s mother tried everything she could to force her daughter to deny the whole story. She continually accused her daughter of lying and deceiving all the people who started coming to the alleged site of the apparition.

Her mother' s attitude and the scorn of her sisters were terribly hard for Lucia to bear. She suffered greatly because she was used to endearments and warmth. With a heavy heart; she spent long hours with her cousins near the well, kneeling in prayer and constantly repeating:"My God! It is for the atonement of sins and the conversion of sinners that we offer you all this suffering and sacrifice. On the 13th June, the parish was celebrating the Feast of St. Anthony, the patron saint of Portugal. From the early hours of the morning, a group of people was waiting outside the house to go with Lucia to Cova da Iria. Lucia invited them all to go with her to 8 o'clock Mass, and only towards 11 o'clock did she call for Jacinta and Francisco at her uncle's house and begin to make her way to Cova da Iria. After the rosary, the little shepherds saw that strange light that they first thought was a flash of lightning. Immediately the white figure appeared above the holm oak. Like in the first vision, it was Lucia who spoke to Our Lady:

"What do you want me to do", she asked. "I want you to come here on the 13th of next

The well near Lucia's house, called Arneiro.

month, say the rosary every day and learn to read. Then I will tell you what I want."
Lucia asked her to heal a sick person.
"If he converts, he will be healed this year". "I would like to ask You to bring us to heaven. "Yes, I will bring Jacinta and Francisco to heaven soon. But you will stay down here for a while yet. Jesus needs you to make the whole world aware of me and love me. He

wants to establish in the world devotion to my Immaculate Heart." "And will I have to stay here all alone?" Lucia asked, sadly.

"No, child. Will you suffer so much? Do not be sad. I will never leave you. My Immaculate Heart will be your refuge and the path that will lead you to God."

Lucia describes the last part of the vision as follows: "As she said these words, she opened her hands and we were bathed in the reflection of Her immense light for the second time. In that light it was as if we were immersed in God. Jacinta and Francisco seemed to be standing in the light that went up to heaven and I seemed to be standing in the light that shone on the earth. Before the palm of Our Lady's right hand there was a heart surrounded by thorns which seemed to pierce it. We understood that it was the Immaculate Heart of Mary, offended by the sins of humanity and desiring atonement."

The little shepherds returned to the village with the people who had prayed with them in Cova da Iria. Everyone questioned them, but they only referred to Mary's request that they say the rosary daily without revealing that part of the vision that concerned their own destiny.

In Aljustrel and the surrounding area, no one spoke of anything else but the little shepherds. Most people mocked them, treating their accounts as the fruit of childish imaginations. Their parents, worried at the way the situation was developing, decided to go and see the parish priest in Fatima, Dom Manuel Ferreira, to ask his advice. Maria Rosa brought her daughter to the presbytery hoping thus to relieve herself of the responsibility of events which she did not understand and whose weight she could no longer bear. The priest questioned Lucia and finally declared, "It does not seem to me to be a revelation from heaven. When these visions occur, Our Lord usually sends those souls he has communicated with to account for what has happened to their confessors or parish priests. Instead, this soul here has retreated into herself as much as possible. This too could be the work of the devil. We will see. The future will reveal what we must think". Lucia was terribly upset and tormented by the thought that the visions could be considered the work of Satan dragging them down to hell. She was assailed by doubts and only Jacinta tried to comfort her saying, "But no, it is not the devil. They say the devil is so ugly, he stays underground in Hell. That Lady is so beautiful and we have seen her ascend to heaven!" Jacinta' s naive reasoning did not convince Lucia, who decided not to return to Cova da Iria. She announced her decision to her cousins on the eve of the 13th July. Her cousins were in

Jacinta and Francisco 's parents: Manuel Pedro Marto and Olimpia de Jesus.

despair because they did not want to go to the site of the apparitions without her. When the day came however, as if drawn by an inner force, she went to collect her cousins and the three of them set off for Cova da Iria. This time, Jacinta and Francisco's father went with them as there was already a crowd of three thousand people in the village. Most of the people were saying the rosary but in the crowd, there were also policemen in plainclothes sent to control the situation. About midday Our Lady appeared, preceded as always by an extraordinary light. She asked the children to return on the 13th of the following month and to say prayers in honour of Our Lady of the Rosary in order to bring about the end of the war. Lucia begged "the vision" to reveal her identity and to perform a miracle to convince everyone of the truth of the visions. In reply, Lucia was assured that the miracle would take place in October. Then "the Lady" asked the children to make sacrifices for the conversion of sinners and to say this prayer: "O Jesus, we make sacrifices for Your love, for the conversion of sinners and to expiate sins committed against the Immaculate Heart of Mary."

What happened afterwards has been called "the secret of Fatima". At the time, the little shepherds told no one what happened in that part of the vision. Many years later, Lucia, urged by the Bishop, described part of that secret. Here is a fragment of her letter: "The reflection seemed to penetrate the earth and we saw something resembling a sea of fire. Immersed in this fire were devils and souls like transparent black or bronze-coloured embers with human features. They rose and fell in the fire, lifted up by the very flames that came from them with clouds of smoke and landing everywhere like sparks flying from huge fires, without weight or balance. The air was full of horrific shouts and moans of despair which had us trembling with fear. (It must have been the shock of that vision that made me gasp 'Aaah', as heard by the watching crowd). The devils had horrible, disgusting features like unknown fearsome animals, but they too were transparent like live black coals. Terrified and, as if to beg Her help, we lifted our eyes to Our Lady, who told us with kindness and sadness: 'You have seen hell, where the souls of poor sinners go. In order to save them, God wishes to spread devotion to the Immaculate Heart all over the world. If they do what I tell you, many souls will be saved and there will be peace on earth. The war will end[*]. But, if they do not stop offending God, another, even worse war will break out during the reign of Pius XI[**].

When you see a night illuminated by an extraordinary light,[***] you will know that it is a great sign of warning sent

---

* The First World War.
** The Second World War began during the reign of Pius XII but the prologue to the war - the annexing of the Sudetenland and later of Bohemia and Moravia - took place during the pontificate of Pius XI.
*** An extraordinary light appeared on the night of the 25th January 1938.

Lucia with her cousin.

by God because he is going to punish the world for its crimes of war, famine and the persecution of the Church and the Holy Father. To avoid this, I will come to beg the consecration of Russia to my Immaculate Heart and the atoning communion of the first Saturday in the month. If they heed my requests, Russia will convert and there will be peace. If not, they will spread their errors throughout the world, provoking wars and the persecution of the Church. The good will be martyred, the Holy Father will suffer greatly and many nations will be destroyed. Finally my Immaculate Heart will triumph. The Holy Father will consecrate Russia to me, the country will be converted and there will be a period of peace in the world. In Portugal the dogma of the faith will always be preserved, ... You must tell no-one what I have told you . Only Francisco, yes, you may tell him'. At this point, the account stops because it has reached the third part of the secret which Lucia did not reveal to anyone, even the Bishop. The third part, written down by her in the years 1943-44, was kept by the Bishop and given to Pope John XXIII in 1958. The Pope did not consider it right to make it public, and from then on, it has been kept in the Vatican archives. It must be explained that Lucia did not reveal the whole content of the apparitions because she herself decided not to, but because of the will of Our Lady.

At the end of the third vision, Mary taught the children the following prayer: "Jesus, forgive us! Save us from the fires of hell and bring all the poor souls to heaven, especially those that have most need."

After Our Lady had disappeared, the crowd surrounded the children. Everyone had heard Lucia*s questions and her cry "Aaah" probably in re-

action to the vision of hell, but they did not know what Our Lady had replied. Lucia told everyone the message of the vision, except for the part concerning the secret which was not revealed for 25 years, and thus not until the end of 1941, when she descibed it in the above-mentioned letter to the Bishop.

The great number of visitors who wished to see and speak with the children, and conflict within the family caused the isolation of the little shepherds. Lucia and her cousins did everything they could to avoid contact with the curious crowds. They preferred to reflect in solitude on what had been revealed to them and this was not easy for them as witnessed by the following conversation between the cousins. Jacinta was tormented by the idea of hell and questioned Lucia:

"That Lady also said that many souls go to hell!
What is hell?"

"It is a hole full of animals with a big big fire (this is how my mother explained it to me) and anyone who sins and does not go to confession, goes there and the fire burns forever and ever."

"And can nobody ever leave there?"

"No."

"And even after many, many years?"

"No, hell never ends."

"And does heaven never end either?" "Anyone who goes to heaven never leaves there."

'And can anyone who goes to hell ever leave?" "Can you not understand that they are eternal, that they never end!"

In this way the children, for the first time, were led to reflect on death and eternity. Jacinta was so upset by the vision of the sinners in hell that she made sacrifices for them every day. Prayer and penance to save souls from the fires of hell became the sole purpose in the life of this eight year old ascetic who received special grace from God. The children's first sacrifice was fasting. At the beginning they gave their bread to the sheep, but afterwards they decided to give it to poor beggars. But it was not easy to keep going all day on an empty stomach, so the children ate what they could find in the fields, acorns, pine-nuts, roots and mushrooms. Jacinta, who was always seeking ways of making sacrifices, proposed that they abstain from drinking. During the summer, this was a real torture that the children bore with great simplicity and humility. One day, Lucia discovered that the cord tied around her waist was hurting her. Imitating Lucia, the little shepherds found another penance, they wore a rope, usually knotted, under their clothes. Jacinta suffered so much that the pain brought tears to her eyes, but she did not remove the cord. She

---

Vila Nova de Ourém: the town hall.

would say: "I want to offer this sacrifice to Jesus in atonement for sins and for the conversion of sinners."

During one of their many interviews, a priest advised the little shepherds to pray for the Holy Father. He explained to them who he was and how he needed the prayers of the faithful. From that day onwards, Jacinta, filled with genuine love for the Pope, added three "Hail Marys" at the end of the rosary for the intentions of the Holy Father. How touching are Jacinta' s words cited by Lucia in her memoirs: "How I would love to see the Holy Father! So many people come here, but the Holy Father has never come to Aljustrel!"

Francisco, unlike his sister who meditated on hell, was completely taken by the vision of God and in particular by the image of Jesus, offended and sad. One day he said to Lucia: "I liked seeing the Angel; but I loved seeing Our Lady even more. But what I loved best was seeing Our Lord in that light that Our Lady put in our hearts. I love God so much! But He is so sad because of all the sins. We must not commit even one ourselves." Francisco was taciturn and liked to pray and do penance alone. He had the gift of meditation and spent long hours praying. When asked what he was doing, he replied: "I am thinking of God who is very sad because of all the sinners. If only I could console Him!"

The children spent their days carrying out their usual chores and above all in prayer and penance. Unfortunately however, more and more people came to Aljustrel to meet the children and hear their story. The children, whenever they could, hid to avoid the continual questioning. Even their parents were worried about the situation being created around their children. Lucia' s mother accused her of making it all up and her sisters radically changed their attitude towards her. As if this was not enough, the people coming to the village thronged onto the piece of land belonging to the dos Santos family, so much so that it was no longer possible to grow either vegetables or corn. Lucia's mother blamed her for this, saying: "Now when you want to eat, go and ask that Lady for something!" The family situation deteriorated even further when Lucia' s father began to go to taverns and drink. Lucia suffered greatly but saw the will of God in everything. The little shepherds did not realise that "the events in Fatima" had been widely reported in the Portuguese press. The Catholic newspapers, as always in such cases, advised prudence and far-sightedness. The liberal and Masonic press mocked the illiterate little shepherds who took in the gullible crowds and accused the Church of organising this "farce" to stir up the people against the republican author ties. Some journalists insinuated that the "apparitions" were nothing but clever publicity stunts to attract attention to the mineral water springs in the area. Consequently the local authorities decided to intervene. On the morning of the 13th August, Arturo de Oliviera Santos, mayor of Vila Nova de Ourém, capital of the region to which Fatima belonged, arrived in Aljustrel. He went directly to the parish priest and had the children brought to him. Then he offered to bring them in his car to the site of the apparitions.

On the way there, he tried to convince the little shepherds to turn back. When the children refused, he lost heart, and instead of bringing them to Cova da Iria, he brought them to his house in Vila Nova de Ourém. All three stayed in the mayor' s house until the following day, cared for by his wife, who fed them and even allowed them to play with their children. In the meantime, a huge crowd was waiting for the "visionaries" at Cova da Iria. Many, many people had come from distant places to take part in this extraordinary event. Everyone took at least one leaf from the tree of the visions and in no time the tree was stripped bare. Many pious people, heedless of the hot summer sunshine, prayed and sang Marian hymns. About midday the disappointed crowd began to get restless, but disappointment turned to rage when rumour spread that the mayor had kidnapped the children. Punc-

Cova da Iria, 13th October 1917.

tually, at twelve o'clock, a clap of thunder was heard. Directly afterwards, a small, luminous cloud appeared above the oak and vanished again almost immediately. Everyone knew that Our Lady had come to meet the little shepherds. Meanwhile the children, who would not deny their "lies", were arrested and thrown into prison, their gaolers even threatening them with boiling oil. Jacinta, terrified, began to cry because she did not want to die without saying goodbye to her mother. Francisco, on the other hand, waited patiently for death, knowing it would bring him closer to heaven as "the Lady" had promised. The prison was in the cellars of the Town Hall and normally held petty thieves and tramps. These tough people, well used to the hardships of prison life, tried to convince the children to reveal "the secret" to the mayor, maintaining that it was not worth spending time in prison. How great was their astonishment when they heard little Jacinta' s categorical reply, "No, I could not do that, I would rather die !" Despite the fears and emotions of that terrible day, the children had not forgotten the rosary. Jacinta asked one of the prisoners to hang her medal on a hook in the wall and all three of them knelt down to say the rosary. This scene so affected the other prisoners that they too joined in the saying of the rosary.

Who knows how many years had passed since those people last turned to God! When the prayers were over, one of the prisoners began to play the accordian and another invited Jacinta to dance. Unfortunately the child was so small that he had to take her in his arms.

The mayor, meanwhile, was trying another plan. He had Dr Antonio Rodrigues de Oliviera brought from Leiria. The psychiatrist was to claim that the children had a tendency to hallucinate. How great was the mayor' s disappointment when the doctor announced that his small patients did not suffer from any mental disorder whatsoever. And so Arturo de Oliviera Santos had no choice but to bring the little shepherds back to Aljustrel, where everyone welcomed them with cries of joy. The children resumed their former way of life, tending the family sheep, and everything seemed back to normal. But, on the 19th August, an extraordinary thing happened. This is how Lucia described the events of that day: "I was bringing the sheep to a place named Valinhos with Francisco and his brother João and I felt something supernatural drawing near us and enveloping us. Thinking that Our Lady was about to appear to us, and not wanting Jacinta to miss her, we asked João to go and call her. Since he did not want to go, we gave him two farthings and he went running off. In the meantime, Francisco and I saw the reflection of the light, that we called the flash of lightning. Jacinta arrived and a moment later we saw Our Lady above a holm oak. 'What do you want me to do?' 'I want you to continue to go to Cova da Iria on the 13th of the month and say the rosary every day. I will perform a miracle on the last month so that everyone will believe.'

'What do you want us to do with the money that people leave in Cova da Iria?'

'We will make two alms boxes. You will carry one with Jacinta and two other girls dressed in white. Francisco and three other boys will carry the other one. The money in the alms boxes is for the Feast of Our Lady of the Rosary. Any money over will go towards the building of a chapel which you will have erected in my honour.

'I would like to ask you to heal some sick people.' 'Yes, I will heal some of them this year.' Her face then became very sad and she said, 'Pray, pray a lot, and make sacrifices for the sake of sinners, as many souls go to hell because there is no-one to make sacrifices and pray for them.' And, as always, she began to rise towards the East."

The visions attracted more and more people all the time. The dos Santos and Marto homes were crowded with devout people who wanted to hear the children's story directly from them, people in despair who wanted the children to pray for a solution to

The crowd waiting for the apparition of Our Lady (13th October 1917).

their own problems and idle onlookers coming to satisfy their curiousity. There were also priests sent by the Church authorities to discreetly follow events in Fatima and, as always in these cases, journalists looking for sensational scoops. It is not surprising therefore that the continual visits and persistent questioning had become a hard penance for the children and it was difficult for them to get away and pray and meditate in solitude.

The day of the next apparition of "the Lady" drew nearer in

People watching the so-called "miracle of the sun".

an atmosphere of increasing tension. On the 13th September, a crowd of twenty, if not thirty thousand people gathered at Cova da Iria. Never before had there been so many people in that part of the country.

Everyone prayed, awaiting the children. In the words of Lucia: "When the hour was nigh, I went with Jacinta and Francis-co, and so many others that we could barely walk. The streets were thronged with people who wanted to see us and talk to us. There was a total absence of human respect. Many many people, including even lords and ladies, managed to make their way through the crowd pressing around us and knelt before us, begging us to present their

supplications to Our Lady. Others, who could not get near to us, shouted from afar: 'For the love of God! Ask Our Lady to heal my son, he's a cripple!' 'May she heal mine, he's blind!' 'Mine, he's blind!' 'Mine, he's deaf!' 'May she bring back my husband and son from the war!' 'May she convert a sinner.' 'May she give me back my health, I'm consumptive.' And so on.

All the misfortunes and distress of the human condition were there before us and some had even climbed onto treetops and walls to call out to us and watch us go by. Saying yes to some and giving our hands to others to help them rise from the dusty earth, we made our way through thq crowd only thanks to some men who opened a path for us through the throngs of people. When I read certain passages now from the New Testament, in particular the fascinating scenes describing when Our

---

Cova da Iria: the moment of the apparition.

Lord travelled through Palestine, I am reminded of those scenes in the poor streets and byways of Aljustrel, Fatima and Cova da Iria, which Our Lord let me take part in, while I was still so young. And I give my thanks to God, offering Him the faith of our good Portuguese people. And I think, if these people humiliated themselves so much before three poor children, just because they had been mercifully conceded the grace to speak to the Mother of God, what would these same people have done if they had seen Jesus Christ before them in person?

However, all this has nothing to do with my story. It is just my pen digressing and leading me somewhere I did not intend to go. Never mind! It is just a worthless extra that I won't cross out so as not to ruin the exercise book.

We finally arrived in Cova da Iria, near the holm oak and began to say the rosary with the people. Shortly afterwards we saw the reflection of the light and, straight away, Our Lady on the oak tree. 'Continue to say the rosary, to bring an end to the war. In October, Our Lord will also come, as well as Our Lady of the Sorrows and Carmine and St. Joseph with the Holy Child, to bless the world. God is satisfied with your sacrifices but He does not want you to sleep with the rope. Wear it only during the day.

"I have been begged to ask you many things, the healing of the sick, a deaf-mute".

"Yes, I will heal some of them, but not all. In October I will perform a miracle so that everyone will believe." And she began to elevate and disappeared as usual".

In the crowd following the apparition, there were two exceptional witnesses, a professor of theology, Dom Manuel Nunes Formigao, sent by the Lisbon Patriarchate, and a young seminarist, Joseph Galamba de Oliviera, future Bishop of Leiria. The latter noticed a luminous sphere moving in the firmament before the apparition. Afterwards white petals began to rain down from the heavens, but as the people stretched out their hands to take them they disappeared about a couple of metres from the ground. During the visions the oak tree where the children stood was enveloped in a white mist and, at the same time, the sun's intensity diminished. Dom Formigao also noticed the change of light, but he interpreted it as being probably a natural phenomenon. In order to study the events in Fatima in more detail, he decided to stay in the area and got lodgings with the Gonçales family in Montelo. First of all, he began to gather all the facts directly from the children and their families. While he was carrying out his enquiries he was struck by the humility of the little shepherds who told their story with great simplicity, avoiding exaggeration and playing down their role in these great events. It is worth mentioning that Father Formigao, under the pseudonym of the Viscount of Montelo, published a very well documented account of the apparitions several years later. It is one of the most interesting books on the events in Fatima. The little shepherds waited calmly for the next encounter with Our Lady, trusting in Her completely. On the contrary, their families were extremely worried and feared for the safety of their children. The people

in the surrounding area were very suspicious and even hostile towards the children. Lucia and her cousins were often threatened and intimidated. As if this was not enough, the Masonic and anticlerical newspapers did everything they could to make the event as public as possible. They were hoping that in this way everyone would discover "the great clerical intrigue" in Fatima. There were rumours that a bomb had been planted under the oak tree. Some priests even sent telegrams to the papers explaining that the visions were merely the result of childish fantasy. Lucia's mother, Maria Rosa, seeing that her daughter would not deny "her lies", had decided to go to the site of the apparitions with her. She said to her daughter, "Lucia, we must go to confession. Everyone says that we will die tomorrow in Cova da Iria... If the Lady does not perform a miracle, the people will kill us. We had better go to confession and prepare ourselves for death."

The woman's surprise was great when she heard her daughter's resolute reply: "I will go to confession with you Mother, but not for this reason. I am not afraid. I know that the lady will do everything she has promised."

On the 12th October a crowd of over thirty thousand people gathered at Cova da Iria. They were prepared to spend the night under the stars.

From dawn onwards on the

following day other people made their way to the site of the apparitions. Journalists estimated the number of people present to be around seventy thousand! About eleven o'clock it began to rain, but although everyone's clothes were wet through, they all stayed waiting for the little shepherds. Here is part of Lucia's account of the events of the 13th October: "We left the house fairly early in view of the slowness of our pace. The village people had turned out en masse. The rain was torrential. My mother, fearing that this was to be the last day of my life and heartbroken with the uncertainty of what was going to happen, wanted to come with me. On the way, there were the same scenes' as on the previous month, even more numerous and moving. Not even the mud on the road stopped those people from kneeling down in the most humble and imploring attitudes. When we got to Cova da Iria, close to the holm oak, inspired by an inner force, I asked the people to close their umbrellas so that we could say the rosary. Shortly afterwards we saw the reflection of the light and straight away Our Lady appeared above the holm oak. 'What do you want me to do?' 'I want you to have a chapel built here in my honour because I am Our Lady of the Rosary, and I want you all to say the rosary every day. The war will end and the soldiers will soon come back home.

'I have many things to ask you, to heal sick people and convert sinners.

'Some yes and others no. They must mend their ways and ask forgiveness for their sins', and her face grew sad, 'They must no longer offend Our Lord God, who has already been greatly wronged' And she opened her hands and they reflected the sun, and as she rose in the air, the reflection of her own light continued to project itself against the sun. This, most reverend Grace, is the reason I cried out to the people to look at the sun. My aim was not to call the people's attention over there because I was no longer aware of their presence. I did it only because I was led to by an inner impulse."

Unfortunately, in all that crowd, only the three little shepherds could see the visions described by Lucia. But everyone was witness to the extraordinary phenomenon that accompanied the visions. First they could see the small white cloud above the holm oak, then afterwards they heard Lucia, inspired by an inner impulse, call out: "Look at the sun" and the clouds instantly disappeared, the rain stopped and the sun came out, a silvery sun which did not blind the eyes. Suddenly the sun started to spin rapidly, emitting different coloured rays in all directions. This phenomenon was repeated three times in front of the astonished crowd who cried "A miracle! A miracle!" A second later, the sun zigzagged downwards and seemed to fall to the ground. "The dance of the sun" - this is what the people called this miraculous phenomenon which lasted ten minutes - had a huge impact on the crowd. Some knelt down beseeching God, others confessed their sins or addressed their supplications to Our Lady. When the sun returned "to its place", the spectators, still shook by the prodigious event, noticed that their soaking wet clothes had inexplicably dried completely. Simple peasants and journalists, quiet middle-class people who had travelled from the capital and fishermen from the Atlantic coast, priests and children, scientists and illiterate people, all babbled together, repeating that this was a sign from heaven, that Our Lady really had appeared to three little shepherds in that remote corner of Portugal to send a message of mercy and salvation to all humanity. "The dance of the sun" was not only seen by people in Fatima. It is worth quoting Laurenço, a boy who was living in a village called Alburitel: "At the time, I was nine years old and went to school in my village, 18 km from Fatima. About midday, we could hear voices out in the street. Our teacher, Delfina Pereira Lopez, a good pious woman but timid and fearful, ran outside. All the pupils followed her. Out in the street people were shouting and crying, pointing at the sun and unable to reply to the teacher's questions. This was a miracle, a great miracle which we saw clearly from the hill on which my village stands. I am unable to describe the phenomenon that took place then. I looked at the sun which seemed pale and did not blind my eyes, it was like a snowball turning on its own axis. Suddenly it began to zigzag downwards and I felt it would fall to the ground. Terrified, I hid among the people. Everyone was crying, expecting the end of the world. Near me stood an unbeliever, all morning he had been laughing at the people leaving for Fatima to "see the Children." I looked at him, he was paralysed with fear, his eyes fixed on the ground. Then he began to tremble violently, he knelt in the mud and, with his hands outstretched, cried: "Our Lady! Our Lady!" Once the apparitions were over, the huge crowd surrounded the little shepherds. Everyone wanted to see them, talk to them and even touch them. Francisco managed to escape and got home in peace. Little Jacinta, lost in that human tide, began to cry, and only thanks to the help of a strong man, was able to get back to her parents who were waiting for her on the roadside. But Lucia remained in the arms of the thousands of people who took her veil, tore her clothes and even cut off her plait.

The visionaries of Fatima.

People stayed in Cova da Iria until late in the evening, praying near the oak tree of the visions. The Viscount of Montelo, privileged witness of the visions and their historian, was waiting for the children in Aljustrel.

Francisco, Jacinta and Lucia, who had not yet had the opportunity to speak to one another were questioned separately.

The three accounts of the apparitions were identical and coincided in every detail.

The children's lives after the Apparitions

The Viscount of Montelo was only one of the hundreds of people who visited the houses of the children. These constant visits actually became a nuisance for the children, who never felt at ease in their roles as leading players in the events which the whole of Portugal was talking about. Whenever possible, they escaped to the hills to pray in the caves.

Crowd upon crowd of pilgrims descended on Cova da Iria, with prayers and supplications for Our Lady. The situation became intolerable for the local authorities, who, in an attempt to keep the people away from this sacred place, even resorted to certain acts of mischief. One night, "someone" destroyed the wooden arch mounted with a cross, which had been erected at Cova da Iria. On another occasion, rumour had it that the oak tree of the visions had been cut down. Lucia immediately ran to see if the news was true and with great relief noted that the wrong tree had been felled. As if this was not enough, the whole area was watched over by soldiers who, not infrequently, told the village children that they would be shot if they did not stay away, in order to frighten them off.

The situation even began to take its toll on Fatima's parish priest, who was totally unable to control the situation. One day he put it plainly to Lucia: "Why do all these people go and prostrate themselves in prayer in the middle of these fields, while the living God, the sworn God of our altars, lies abandoned and alone in the tabernacle? What is all this money for? This money that serves no purpose, left under the holm oak while we cannot finish the construction of our church for want of funds!"

Then, Lucia's mother fell seriously ill and the child had to put up with the taunting of her sisters who accused her of being the cause of the illness. They even challenged her faith by sending her to Cova da Iria to ask Our Lady for Maria Rosa's recovery. How great must have been Lucia's pain, accused as she was of having brought on her mother's suffering! In tears, she ran to the hillside where she prayed desperately to Our Lady, promising that she would crawl on her knees as far as the oak tree of the miracles if her Heavenly Mother were to grant her earthly mother the grace of a recovery. Three days later, Maria Rosa already felt much improved and soon she was completely recovered. To fulfill her vow, Lucia, together with her sisters, went to say the rosary every day for nine days at the holm oak, crawling

Francisco 's tomb at the cemetery in Fatima.

on their knees for the last part of the way. It was at that time the children also started going to the school in Fatima to learn how to read and write, as Our Lady had requested them. Every morning, on their way to school, they stopped off in the church to pray to the Most Holy. Francisco often stayed on, explaining to the others, "You go on to school, I'm staying here with the Hidden Jesus". He would spend the whole morning consoling "Jesus, who is so sad" and praying for everything the people asked him to pray for. After school the children returned home and performed the household chores their parents gave them. Lucia no longer looked after her flock, which was sold off, except for three lambs which remained in the sheep pen beside the house. She also learned to cook and weave at that time.

At this point the words of St. Luke come to mind when he thus described the infant Jesus: "...then he went down with them and came to Nazareth ... And Jesus increased in wisdom and in years, and in divine and human favour" (Lk 2, 51-52). The simple life of the Children of Fatima was an unending prayer and hymn to God. In 1917 the war ended and peace returned to a devastated Europe. Unfortunately, an influenza epidemic broke out in Portugal which decimated the population, already exhausted after the war. At the end of 1918 Francisco and Jacinta fell ill, together with other members of their family. Their father - the only one who resisted the 'flu - had to look after his wife and children. Lucia often went to visit her cousins, without thought for the fact that she could be at risk from contagion. Unfortunately, however, her cousins' state of health worsened, as pneumonia followed influenza. For both of them, their Calvary had commenced. The illness, which would be the last stage of their short lives and which would bring them to meet Jesus and His Immaculate Mother, was another occasion for penitence.

During his illness Francisco was always calm and serene. One day he confessed to Lucia, "I am in pain, but it doesn't matter. I am suffering to console Our Lord, and I'll be in heaven shortly". When his health permitted, Francisco made his way to Cova da Iria, knelt down by the oak tree and said a rosary aloud. Our Lady's words were always in his mind: "Francisco will go to heaven, but he will have to say many rosaries". Every moment was spent in prayer and therefore to bring him always one step nearer to Jesus. He even stopped playing so as not to lose time. He met many kind people who promised to pray for his health. He replied, with the calmness of one who knows his own destiny, "Your prayers for my health are useless, I will never have the grace of recovery!" And he was ght. His condition worsened notably in February. He began to suffer from terrible headaches. Sometimes he was so weak he could not pronounce the words of his prayers. His mother advised him to say his rosary in his head, telling him "Our Lady looks into our hearts and will be content all the same".

At that time the boy removed the cord which he had been using to do penance; he was afraid his mother would discover it. Jacinta and Lucia spent all their free time with Francisco. One day, early in the morning, Francisco asked to see Lucia. When his cousin arrived, he told her "I need to go to confession so I can have communion before I die. I want you to tell me if you have seen me commit any sin and then go to Jacinta and ask if she, too, has seen me do anything". Lucia listed all his little sins as far as she could remember; he had disobeyed his mother at times, he had stolen ten centavos from his father to buy a harmonica, he had thrown stones at the boys

Identification of the mortal remains of Jacinta (1952).

from the next village. Francisco thanked his cousin, adding "Maybe it's because of these sins that I made Our Lord so sad. But, even if I don't die, I will never do those things again, now that I have repented. Oh, my Jesus! Forgive us! Save us from the fires of hell, bring all the poor souls to heaven, especially those that have most need". That evening, the priest confessed him, promising that he would return to give him Holy Communion. The next day, after taking Communion, Francisco was radiant with joy and said to Jacinta, "Today I am happier than you, because the Hidden Jesus is inside me".

On the last evening Lucia said farewell to her cousin, saying "Goodbye, Francisco! If you reach heaven tonight, don't forget me up there". "I won't forget you", he replied. Jacinta instead asked him to pass on 'her dear greetings to Our Lord and his Holy Mother" and to "tell them that I will suffer all they want for the sake of the Immaculate Heart of Mary and for the conversion of sinners". Then they bade each other farewell, saying, "See you in heaven!".

Jacinta and Francisco had had another apparition during their illness. This is how Jacinta described it to Lucia: "Our Lady came to see us, to tell us that she would soon be coming to fetch Francisco and take him to heaven. She asked me if I wanted to convert more sinners and I said I did. Then she told me that I would go to hospital and would suffer greatly there. She told me to suffer for the conversion of sinners, as penance for the sins against the Immaculate Heart of Mary and for the sake of Jesus. I asked her if you would be with me. She said no. That is the worst thing. She said my mother would come to take me but that I would be alone there. If only you could come too! The most difficult thing will be going without you! And maybe the hospital will be dark, and I won't be able to see anything, and I'll be there all alone, suffering! But it doesn't matter. I'll be suffering for Our Lord, to make amends for the wrong done to the Immaculate Heart of Mary, for the conversion of sinners and for the Holy Father".

On the morning of Friday 4th April 1919, Olimpia was alone watching over her son. Suddenly, Francisco said to her "Mama, look over there, near the door! Can you see that beautiful light?" Who knows if it was the same light that he had seen at Cova da Iria. Then he added, "I can't see it any more", and with a smile on his lips, he flew into the arms of the One he had been privileged to see during his life. Today he is surely consoling Jesus, whom he loved so much on earth. Francisco Marto was buried without a coffin in the cemetery at Fatima. In 1952 his mortal remains were exhumed, identified and moved to a side altar in the basilica.

Jacinta's calvary

The death of her brother was a hard blow for Jacinta as she had lost the one person with whom she had shared everything during his short life and to whom she was joined by the great mystery of the visions. Jacinta, like Francisco, had the "Spanish influenza". This was a dangerous strain of influenza which had spread in an epidemic throughout the world in 1918. But as her brother's illness was more serious, she suffered in silence so as not to give her mother any more cause for worry. More or less a year after the apparitions, Jacinta was struck by bronchitis, which was followed by pneumonia. She was forced to take to her bed, watched over by her mother, who had to endure seeing her second child in agony. Her mother's tears made her suffer more than her own pain and to console her, Jacinta lied, saying "Mama, don't cry. There's nothing wrong with me". Often, upon seeing the distraught face of her mother, she would say, "Mama, don't torment yourself. I'm going to heaven and I will be able to pray for you there'. Lucia was, as always, Jacinta's only confidant. One day Lucia asked her cousin if she was in great pain. "Not at all! I am offering everything I have for the sake of the Immaculate Heart of Mary and for sinners", replied Jacinta. On another occasion she said, "How I love to suffer for the sake of Our Lord and the Blessed Virgin, to please them.

They love everyone who suffers for the conversion of sinners". In July 1919, the doctors advised the Marto family to bring Jacinta to Vila Nova de Ourém where she would be nearer the hospital. The young patient stayed there for two months. Her mother, Olimpia, visited her frequently and brought Lucia on two occasions. Despite the treatment, the girl's condition worsened and a large wound opened in her chest. At the end of August, the doctors decided to send her home. Here is what Lucia had to write about Jacinta's life at that time: "She returned for a while to her own house. There was a large abcess on her chest but she put up with her daily medication with never a complaint, without ever showing the faintest sign of being ill. Most difficult of all were the frequent visits and interviews with people who had been looking for her and from whom she could no longer hide. - This sacrifice too I make for the sake of sinners, -she said with resignation.

- Oh, if only I could make it as far as Cabeço to say one more rosary at our little cave! But it's too late, now. When you go to Cova da Iria, pray for me. I won't be going any more. - And the tears ran down her face.

One day my aunt said to me, "Ask Jacinta what she's thinking about, when she keeps her hands over her face like that for ages, without moving. I have asked her, but she never answers. She just smiles". So I put the question to her and she replied:

- I'm thinking of Our Lord, of the Blessed Virgin, of all the sinners and ... (here she mentioned something about the secret). I love to think".

Every day Lucia visited her sick cousin. Jacinta told her once that she had had a vision of Our Lady. The Virgin had revealed her earthly destiny. "She said I would go to Lisbon, to another hospital but that I would never see my parents again. She said that after long suffering I would die alone, but that I shouldn't be afraid because she would come and carry me to heaven". For Jacinta, the thought of being separated from her family and of dying alone caused her to suffer more than from the physical pain. She often kissed her crucifix and held it to her tightly, saying, "Oh my Jesus, how I love you and how I wish to suffer for you" or "Jesus, now you can convert many sinners, for my sacrifice is great". Another time, Lucia saw her cousin kiss a picture of Our Lady saying, "Dear Heavenly Mother, must I really die alone?". For the patient, the time had come to climb the Mount of Olives, to live her own Gethsemane and she, in the knowledge of her destiny, seemed to be saying as Jesus did, "Father, if you are willing, remove this cup from me; yet, not my will but yours be done" (Lk 22, 42).

In January, Dr. Eurico Lisbôa from the capital, arrived and expressed a desire to see the girl.

Seeing her condition, he tri[e] to convince her parents to l[et] him operate on her in Lisbon. At first, Senhor & Senhora Ma[r]to did not want to let their chi[ld] be taken away to the city. Th[e] doctor insisted, however, sa[y]ing that the operation was h[er] only hope for her survival, a[nd] eventually he obtained the[ir] consent. Jacinta left for Lisbo[n] and thus did the words of O[ur] Lady come true.

Before leaving Aljustrel f[or] good Jacinta wished to visit th[e] site of the apparitions. She w[as] too weak to walk and Olimp[ia] had to borrow a donkey to ta[ke] her daughter to Cova da Iri[a]. The girl, although much wea[k]ened, was able to make the la[st] stretch of road on foot. Sh[e] looked at the houses in the v[il]lage, at the woods, the valle[y] and the hillsides dotted wi[th] caves, at the countryside whi[ch] had been the scene of th[e] greatest moment of her life, her meeting with Our Lady!

On the 21st January 1920, Jaci[n]ta said goodbye to Lucia for th[e] last time: "We will never se[e] each other again. Pray for m[e] until I go to heaven. When I a[m] there, I will pray for you. Neve[r] tell our secret to anyone, n[ot] even if they threaten to kill yo[u]. Yo[u] must love Jesus and the Im[]maculate Heart of Mary and yo[u] must make many sacrifices f[or] the sake of sinners". Olimpi[a] Marto accompanied her daugh[]ter to Lisbon and stayed for [a] few days. However, when th[e] people who had invited he[r] saw the condition of the gir[l] they refused to take her in. Jac[]

inta was eventually put up in an orphanage run by the Order of Our Lady of Miracles, at 17 Rua da Estrela. The director, Sister Maria da Purificação Godinho, looked after the little girl with all her heart and tried to ease her suffering, as the girl's own mother would have. The patient's room was near another room from which you could see the inside of the church with the chapel. In this way she was able to receive the Eucharist every day and spent long hours in prayer, meditating before the "Hidden Jesus". She was visited on occasion by Our Lady, who revealed to her the day and hour of her death. Jacinta confided often in Sister Godinho, saying things which could not possibly have been the fruit of a ten-year-old girl's meditations.

Here are some examples: "If people only knew what eternity was really like, they would do everything possible to change their way of life", "There will come fashions that will offend Our Lord. People who wish to serve God cannot be slaves to fashions. There is no room for fashions in the Church. God is always the same". "The sins which lead many souls to hell are sins of impurity", "Doctors cannot heal the sick because they do not love God", "Priests must be pure, very pure! The disobedience of many priests and clerics towards their superiors and towards the Holy Father displeases Our Lord greatly". On the 2nd February, Jacinta confessed herself, received Communion, said goodbye to the orphanage and left for the Donna Estefania Hospital. The operation took place on the 10th February. The little patient was considered too weak to undergo anaesthesia with chloroform, so the doctors gave her a simple local anaesthetic and the operation was carried out under her gaze. Two ribs were removed from the left-hand side of her body and left a wide cavity. Her bandages had to be changed regularly in the following days; and this proved to be extremely painful for the girl. The staff at the hospital were astounded that she never complained even once and said only, "We must be strong and suffer everything in order to get to heaven". A few days after the operation she was found by one of the nurses, serene and relaxed. When asked how she felt, Jacinta replied that she had had another visit from Our Lady, who had promised that soon she would be in heaven. From that day on, all her physical pain ended. On the 20th February, feeling that she had reached the end of her earthly pilgrimage, Jacinta asked that she be given the sacraments. A priest from a nearby church confessed her promising that he would return the next day with the Eucharist.

That same day, towards ten in the evening, Our Lady entered the hospital in silence to take the little shepherd girl from Aljustrel, the little mystic whom she had chosen as instrument of her presence among men.

Lucia's story

In only a short time, God had called both Francisco and Jacinta. Now Lucia was alone. In her memoirs she wrote about that sad period of her life. "I felt so disconsolate, being alone! In such a short time, the Good Lord had taken away my own dear father, then Francisco and finally Jacinta, and I would never see them again in this world. As soon as I could, I went to Cabeço and entered the cavern in the rock to release my pain and sorrow directly in the presence of God. My tears fell freely. As I came down the slope again, everything reminded me of my dear companions - the rocks we so often sat upon, the flowers I no longer picked, having no-one to bring them to. Valinhos, the place where we had tasted the delights of paradise".

It was in that period that the Bishop of Leiria began to take an interest in Lucia, the last remaining visionary. With her mother's consent, the Bishop sent her to a convent schoöl run by nuns from the Order of St. Dorothy of Vilar, near Porto. Lucia, who was fourteen by now, said goodbye to her relatives with a heavy heart and left the place where she had grown up. At last the day of my departure was decided. The evening beforehand, I went to say farewell to the countryside, sure in the knowledge that I would never walk those hills again Cabeço, the rock, Valinhos, the parish church where the Good Lord had begun His work of mercy, the cemetery where I was leaving behind the mortal remains of my father and of Francisco, who I was unable to forget. I took my leave of our well, already illuminated by moonlight, and of the old farmyard where I had spent many an hour in contemplation of the beautiful, starry sky and the marvels of the sunrises and sunsets which, at times, astounded me, with the sun's rays reflecting in the dew which covered the hills in the morning, like pearls. I remembered, too, the snowflakes in the afternoons when it snowed, how they hung from the pine branches and reminded me of the beauties of heaven .

Lucia left Fatima in secret in order to avoid curious crowds, and above all, the authorities, who had subjected her to traumatic interrogations. On the 17th June she joined the convent school, where she completed her primary schooling. In the same period a religious vocation developed within her. In 1925 she was sent to Pontevedra, in Spain, where the nuns of St. Dorothy had a house. On the 3rd October 1928 she made her first temporary vows and six years later, on the same date, her

Lucia, photo taken just after the apparitions.

perpetual vows. She took the name of Maria Lucia das Dores, that is to say, Maria Lucia of the Sorrows. At that time, Lucia also had several visions of a private nature. In 1927 the sister revealed their content to her confessor, Father José Aparicio da Silva S.J., who instructed her to prepare a written statement on these matters. Feeling a little embarrassed, she decided to write in the third person, as if she had been just an eyewitness to the events. The following is her report: "On the 17th December 1927 she went to the chapel to ask Jesus how she could satisfy the request which had been made of her, given that the origins of her devotion to the Immaculate Heart of Mary lay in the secret confided to her by the Most Holy Virgin.

Jesus, with a clear voice, let her hear these words: 'My child, write what they have asked you to write. You must also write everything which the Most Holy Virgin revealed to you in the vision in which she spoke of this devotion. As far as the rest of the secret is concerned, continue to maintain your silence'. What had been revealed in 1917 in this regard was as follows. She had asked that they be brought to heaven. The Most Holy Virgin replied, 'Yes, I will take Jacinta and Francisco soon, but you will stay down here for a while yet. Jesus needs you to make the whole world aware of me and love me. He wants to establish in the world devotion to my Immaculate Heart. To whomsoever embraces it, I promise salvation, and these souls will be dear to God, like the flowers with which I decorate his throne'.

- Will I have to stay here alone? - she said sadly.

- No, child. I will never leave you. My Immaculate Heart will be your refuge and the path that will lead you to God.

On the 10th December 1925, the Most Holy Virgin appeared to her with a boy in a bright cloud at her side. Resting one hand on His shoulder, the Most Holy Virgin showed her a heart which was in her other hand. The heart was surrounded by thorns. Then the boy said, "Have pity on the heart of your Most Holy Mother, which is covered with thorns which constantly pierce it due to the actions of ungrateful man and there is no-one who makes any act of penance to remove the thorns". Shortly afterwards the Most Holy Virgin said, "Look, my child, at my Heart, surrounded by thorns with which selfish men constantly pierce me, with blasphemy and ingratitude. At least you, of all people, must try to console me, and tell all of them that on the first Saturday of each of the next five months they should confess themselves and receive Holy Communion. They should say a rosary and keep me company for a quarter of an hour, meditating on the fifteen mysteries of the rosary, in order to give me relief. I promise then that I will help them at the moment of their death, with all the graces necessary for the salvation of their souls".

On the 15th December 1926, the infant Jesus appeared to her again. He asked her if she had yet spread the devotion to his Most Holy Mother. She explained the difficulty her confessor had had and that her Mother Superior was willing to spread the news, but that the confessor had said that she alone could do nothing. Jesus replied, 'It is true that your superior, alone, can do nothing, but with my grace anything is possible' ".

The next vision took place in the chapel of a religious institution at Tuy on the 13th June 1929. Sister Lucia described it thus: "Father P. Gonçalves came to our chapel sometimes to hear confessions. I confessed to him and as he seemed to understand me, I continued with him for the three years that he remained here as joint provincial.

It was in this period that Our Lady warned me that the time had come for the Holy Church to know of her wish for the consecration of Russia and of her promise to convert it. The communication was as follows: 13th June 1929. I had asked for and obtained permission from my superiors and confessor to have my holy hour from eleven to midnight, on Thursday night. Alone one night, I knelt down between the two parts of the balustrade, in the middle of the chapel, to recite the Angelus. Feeling tired, I got up and continued my prayers with my arms held out to the side. The only light was that which came from the lamp of the Most Holy. Suddenly, the entire chapel was illuminat-

Lucia with the Bishop of Leiria.

ed by a supernatural light and over the altar a cross of light appeared, which reached the roof. In a clearer light the face and upper body of a man could be seen on the upper part of the cross. On his breast was a dove-shaped light, and there was the body of another man nailed to the cross. Just below the belt-line, floating in the air, you could see a chalice and a large Host, upon which fell several drops of blood, running from a wound in the chest and falling onto the face of the crucified man. Slipping off the Host, these drops fell into the chalice. Under the right arm of the cross was Our Lady (it was Our Lady of Fatima, with neither sword nor roses, but with a crown of thorns and flames), with her Immaculate Heart in her hand... Under the left arm of the cross were some large letters, like of crystal-clear water, which ran onto the altar, forming the words: "Grace and Mercy".

I understood that I was being shown the mystery of the Most Holy Trinity and I was given enlightenment on this mystery which I am not allowed to reveal.

Then Our Lady said to me: 'The moment has come for God to ask the Holy Father, in union with the bishops of the whole world, to consecrate Russia to my Immaculate Heart, promising to save it by this means. So many are the souls which God's justice condemns for having sinned against me that I come to ask for amends to be made, You must make sacrifices and pray so that this will come about'. I told this to my confessor, who asked me to write down what Our Lady had asked be done". Later, still in Tuy, Lucia heard the voice of Christ who confirmed that he wanted people to perform acts of devotion on the five Saturdays as penance for the offences and blasphemy against the Immaculate Heart of Mary. He also warned that the day of judgement of all nations was drawing nearer. Then he added: "They have not taken my request into consideration. Like the King of France, they will repent and do what I ask, but it will be too late. Russia will already have spread her errors around the world, provoking wars and persecuting the Church. The Holy Father will have much cause to suffer".

During her stay in Tuy, Sister Lucia wrote her memoirs, as the religious authorities had asked her to. The first collection appeared in 1935, the second in 1937, the third in 1941 and the fourth in December of the same year. After reading the first memoir, Bishop da Silva of Leiria insisted that she also describe the so-called "Secret of Fatima", which was in three parts. The first dealt with wars, hell and punishment for the sins of humanity. The second part spoke of devotion to the Immaculate Heart of Mary. These first two parts were contained in the third collection of Sister Lucia's memoirs. The "third secret", instead, was described over twenty-three pages between the 22nd December 1943 and the 9th January 1944 and was handed over, in a sealed envelope, to the Bishop of Leiria, Monsignor da Silva, who then sent it, by means of the Papal Nuncio, to the Pope. It was then left to the Pope to decide on publication of its contents, according to the wishes of Our Lady.

It should be explained that Sister Lucia was greatly perplexed and did not actually want to write this summary of the third secret, due to its apocalyptic nature. All the popes since then have known the contents of the text, but have not held it opportune to make it public.

Sister Lucia returned to Portugal in May 1946 and so, after many years, she was finally able to see once more her native village, Aljustrel, and the site of the apparitions, Cova da Iria. She soon missed the contemplative life, however, and having obtained the permission of Pope Pius XII, she entered a Carmelite convent in Coimbra on the 25th March 1948, with the name Sister Mary of the Immaculate Heart. To this day (1993) she still lives there, seeking to spread devotion to the Immaculate Heart of Mary, a task entrusted to her by Our Lady, and waiting for the day when God calls her to Him, to be reunited with Francisco and Jacinta.

Lucia with the Superior of the Sisters of St. Dorothy Convent in Tuy.

The Marian Cult in Fatima

Even after the second apparition, Cova da Iria had already become a destination for pilgrims and a place of prayer for the people from the surrounding areas. On the 13th October 1917, the date of the last apparition, a crowd of seventy thousand people, from all over Portugal, gathered there. The site, sanctified by the presence of the Mother of God, was also visited every day by people wanting to recite the rosary. A rough wooden arch surmounted by a cross was erected near the oak tree of the visions and was later replaced by another arch, this time of stone. Later again, a chapel was built at the site and was inaugurated on the 18th April 1919. The country was at that time governed by a clique of freemasons who did not want the Marian cult in Fatima to develop any further. At the time of the third apparition, on the 19th August 1917, anti-clerical circles organized a demonstration with the connivance of the local authorities against the "machinations of the priests". This demonstration turned out to be a fiasco however, despite the best efforts of the organizers. After this, the usual "persons unknown" destroyed the arch at Cova da Iria, together with all the religious articles there, and uprooted an oak, which was, fortunately, not that of Our Lady. As time went by the reaction of the freemasons became ever more violent. Another demonstration, organized at Santarém, was a farsical mock-religious procession where those who took part blasphemed against Our Lady and profaned her sacred image. The priests in Fátima were persecuted by the authorities who decided to ban all public gatherings at Cova da Iria. This anticlerical furore, however, had entirely the opposite effect to that desired. Instead of distancing themselves from a "corrupt Church", people returned to it, having repented. One young man who converted at the time of the visions was Gilberto F. Santos, from the town of Torres Novas. In thanks for graces received, he donated a statue of Our Lady to the Fatima site. It was carved in wood by José Ferreira Thedim, a sculptor from Braga, according to precise instructions provided by the visionaries. The authorities obviously did not wish to permit the placing of a statue in the

Lucia's manuscript containing the first two parts of the "secret of **Fatima**".

que nos disse com bondade e tristeza. Vistes
o inferno, para onde vão as almas dos pobres
pecadores; para as salvar Deus quer estabelecer
no mundo a devoção a meu Imaculado
Coração, se fizerem o que eu vos disser salvar-
se-ão muitas almas e terão paz: a guerra
vai acabar: mas se não deixarem de ofender a
Deus, no reinado de Pio XI começará outra
peor. Quando virdes uma noite alumiada por
uma luz desconhecida, sabei que é o grande
sinal que Deus vos dá de que vai a punir o
mundo de seus crimes, por meio da guerra, da
fome e de perseguições à Igreja e ao Santo Padre.

Para a empedir, virei pedir a consagração da Russia a meu Imaculado Coração, e a Comunhão repa-
radora nos primeiros sabados. Se atenderem a meus
pedidos a Russia se converterá e terão paz: se não,
espalhará seus erros pelo mundo, promovendo guer-
ras e perseguições à Igreja, os bons serão martiri-
zados, o Santo Padre terá muito que sofrer, varias
nações serão aniquiladas: por fim o meu
Imaculado Coração triunfará. O Santo Padre
consagrar-me-á a Russia que se converterá e
será concedido ao mundo algum tempo de
paz. Em Portugal se conservará sempre o dogma da fé etc. Isto não o digais a ninguem.
Ao Francisco sim, podeis dize-lo.

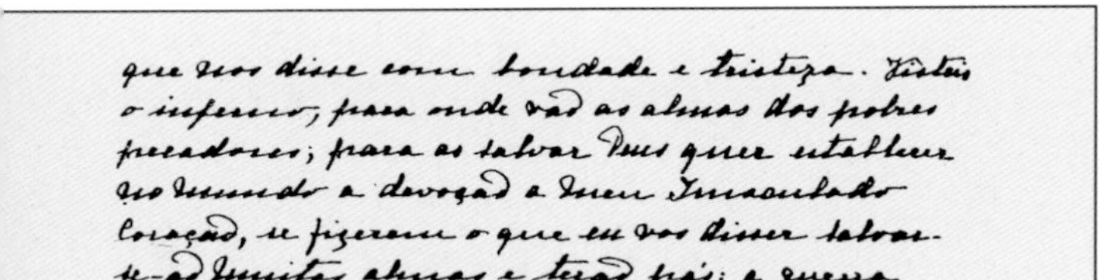

Lucia after the apparitions.

chapel, but were unable to stop the faithful who got around the police control points and carried the figure of the Virgin to the chapel, hidden in a farmworker's cart. The government in Lisbon was becoming more and more preoccupied with events at Fatima. Mayors of the towns in the area surrounding Aljustrel were ordered to organize control points along the roads to stop people from reaching Fatima. The military erected a real roadblock at Cova da Iria, but not even this was enough to cease the flow of pilgrims, who instead had to pass through the fields and woods to avoid the soldiers and police. As they could no longer tolerate this situation, the freemasons resorted to more radical tactics. On the night of the 5th March 1922 the usual "persons unknown" dynamited the chapel with four bombs. A fifth device was placed under the oak tree of the visions, but did not go off. Nor did the figure of Our Lady suffer any damage in the explosion, as the local people used to take her to one of the houses in the village every night. But the problems did not end here.

A fierce campaign was started in the press against the local clergy who were accused of having organized the "farce of Fatima". According to certain journalists, the priests had trained three illiterates in the part of "visionaries", and had even organized their "disappearance". Using the usual anticlerical language, they demanded that the authorities put an end to the actions of these "reactionary conservative forces". In reply to the fury of the powers that be, the people came in ever-increasing numbers to Fatima. On the 13th May 1922, the fifth anniversary of the first apparition, a crowd of sixty thousand gathered at the site to beg Mary's forgiveness for all the offences against her. As is normal in these cases, the ecclesiastical authorities acted somewhat more prudently. First of all, they questioned the children and their families. While waiting for the results of the inquiry, the priests were asked not to participate in gatherings at Cova da Iria. However, as time went on the local bishop, Monsignor Thsé Alves Correia da Silva, reasoned that it was not possible to leave the crowds without pastoral guidance. For this reason he permitted celebration of the Holy Mass for pilgrims as early as October 1921. The following year, the same authorities acquired all the land around Cova da Iria - about 125,000 sq metres in all - so that the site could not be profaned. Unfortunately there was no water in the area for the pilgrims. Imagine then the surprise of certain workmen who started digging in the dry earth when, after the first few blows of their picks, they came across an ample supply of water, so much so that it became known as "the Water of Our Lady". In 1926, the site of the apparitions was visited by the Apostolic Nuncio. The following year, the Bishop of Leiria personally led a pilgrimage to Fatima, inaugurating the fourteen Stations of the Cross, each Station consisting of a large stone cross offered by the surrounding parishes. On the 13th October 1930, after eight years' work by the ecclesiastical commission which had been studying the events at Fatima, the results of the inquiry were published and the Bishop announced them in his pastoral letter: "We hereby:

1) declare creditable the children's visions at Cova da Iria in the Parish of Fatima, in this diocese, on the 13th of each month between May and October 1917.

2) give our official consent to the cult of Our Lady of Fatima". This recognition of the visions on the part of the Church authorities permitted the organization of official pilgrimages. On the 13th May 1931 the first national Portuguese pilgrimage arrived. In a moving ceremony, the bishops declared Portugal to be under the protection of the Immaculate Heart of Mary. It should be explained that the country was in a particularly difficult moment in its history. Communist propaganda was rife and there was a real risk that Portugal become a Soviet state. In 1936 the Bishops met in the Chapel of the Apparitions to beg Our Lady to save the country from the lashes of war and promising a second consecration of Portugal to the Immaculate Heart of Mary. Shortly thereafter, a bloody civil war broke out in neighbouring Spain which caused the deaths of thousands of Spanish priests and nuns, the destruction of churches, chapels and monasteries, and painfully split the nation in two. Portugal, though, was spared this fratricidal fighting. To thank Our Lady for the gift of peace, a series of pilgrimages of thanksgiving were organized in 1938. It seemed that the whole country was marching towards Fatima. Twenty bishops, a thousand priests and with them more than half a million faithful who fell to their knees before the statue of Our Lady, consecrating the country to her protection. The 25th anniversary of the visions was in the year 1942. War was rag-

ing in Europe, bringing death and destruction. St. Peter's Chair was occupied by Pope Pius XII, who liked to be known as the Pope of Fatima. This was also the Jubilee Year for Pius XII, the 25th anniversary of his consecration as bishop which had taken place on the 13th May 1917! On the 13th October the Pope made a radio broadcast, consecrating the entire world to the Immaculate Heart of Mary. The following is an excerpt from the broadcast: "In this tragic hour in the history of man we, as Father of the Christian family, solemnly consecrate to Thee and to Thy Most Holy Heart, the Holy Church, Mystical Body of Thy Son, which suffers and bleeds in many places and forms. We also dedicate to Thee the whole world, torn by cruel discord and victim of its own iniquity". After the war, Pius XII sent a Papal Legate to Fatima to crown the statue of Our Lady Queen of the World and of Peace. Some years later, during the feast of Saints Cyril and Methodius (7th June 1952), the Pope consecrated the peoples of Russia, who were suffering under the atheism of the communist dictatorship, to the Most Holy Heart of Mary with his encyclical "Sacro vergente anno".

In this same period, the parish priest of Plainfield, USA, Fr. Harold Colgan, organized a movement with the aim of combatting atheism - the greatest heresy of all time, as Pius XII called it. This movement had its headquarters at Fatima and was called the "Blue Armada" or the "Armada of Mary" and today has tens of millions of members in over one hundred countries. At the Armada's headquarters in the Byzantine chapel, the world-famous icon of

The chapel erected on the site of the apparitions.

Our Lady of Kazan was given a home. This icon, a symbol of the Christian roots of the Russian people, was probably painted in the 13th century. At the end of the 16th century it was placed in a church built for that purpose in Kazan.

Later it was transported to Moscow where it embellished one of the churches in the Kremlin. In 1721 Peter the Great wanted to bring it to St. Petersburg and in 1811 the Cathedral of Kazan was consecrated there. The icon was considered the most valuable reliquy of the capital city. After the Napoleonic Wars, the icon was transferred back to Kazan, where it remained until the time of the Bolshevic Revolution. During the Civil War it was brought to the United States of America and later again Father Haffer managed to bring it to Fatima and place it in the Blue Armada chapel. Recently a copy of an icon of Our Lady of Czestochowa was hung near that of Kazan.

Pope John XXIII visited Fatima in 1956 while he was still Patriarch of Venice. After his election as Pope he received the text of Sister Lucia's deposition regarding the third secret of Fatima. "The Pope of Peace" was particularly sensitive to the Marian message of Fatima as he had to guide the Church through the period of the Cold War and the ideological expansion of the Soviet Union. Pope Paul VI was the first Pope to visit Fatima, in 1967, on the occasion of the 50th anniversary of the visions. The Pope explained the purpose of his apostolic visit as follows: "So great is our desire to honour the Most Holy Virgin Mary, Mother of Christ and therefore Mother of God and our Mother, so great is her benevolence towards the Holy Church and to Our apostolic office, so great is Our desire for Her intercession with Christ, Her divine Son, that We have come as faithful and humble pilgrims to this blessed Shrine where we commemorate the 25th anniversary of the consecration of the world to the Immaculate Heart of Mary" (from the homily given during the Holy Mass at Fatima, 13th May 1967). The Pope invited Sister Lucia to the ceremony celebrating the 50th anniversary. She was the one visionary who Our Lady had chosen to spread the cult of Her Immaculate Heart.

In 1977 Sister Lucia also met Cardinal Albino Luciani who was to become Pope John Paul I. On the 16th October 1978, after the brief pontificate of John Paul I, the College of Cardinals elected Karol Wojtyla as Bishop of Rome. The new Pope took his predecessor's name of John Paul and as his motto, "Totus tuus" - "All Yours".

Here began the pontificate of the Pope-Apostle of Mary. Precisely on the 64th anniversary of the events at Fatima, on the 13th May 1981, John Paul II fell prey to an attempt on his life. Despite his serious injuries, however, he soon recovered. A year later the Pope came to Fatima: "Because, on this exact day last year in St. Peter's Square, in Rome there was an attempt on the life of your Pope, which mysteriously coincided with the anniversary of the first vision at Fatima, that of the 13th May 1917. The concidence of these dates was so great that it seemed to be a special invitation for me to come here". Unfortunately, on the evening before the first anniversary of the attack, Pope John Paul II was subjected to another attack. This time, a young Spaniard dressed as a priest tried to knife him on the steps of the basilica. His attacker, Juan Fernandez Krohn, managed only to lightly injure one of the Pope's entourage, while shouting: "Enough of this Pope! Enough of Vatican II!". On the 13th May Holy Mass was celebrated in front of a million worshippers. The text of the papal speeches made on the Pontiff's visit are contained in the second part of this book. The Pope met Sister Lucia at Fatima, where he consecrated the world to the Immaculate Heart of Mary. Pope John

Jacinta, photo taken after the last apparition.

Paul II returned for the second time to Fatima on the 13th May 1991 for the 10th anniversary of the attack in St. Peter's Square. On this occasion he said: "I come to kneel once again at the feet of Our Lady of Fatima, giving Her thanks for Her revelation on the path of mankind and of Nations, and for the wonders and blessings which the Almighty has worked in her, appealing to His Omnipotence". The Holy Father also wanted to thank her for having saved his life which, as we have seen, had been put in danger by a fanatical terrorist.

Together with the other pilgrims he recited the rosary in front of the statue of Our Lady and placed the bullet, which had been removed from his body after the attack, in her crown.

He then celebrated Holy Mass consecrating humanity to the Immaculate Heart of Mary.

Cardinal Masella, Papal Legate to Pius XII, crowning the statue of Our Lady of Fatima.

The shrine at Fatima

As has been said already, there was a small chapel on the site of the apparitions as early as 1919, which had been donated by a pious woman, Maria dos Santos Carreira. The first chapel which was destroyed in the explosion of the 6th March 1922, was subsequently replaced by larger constructions which accomodated ever-greater numbers of pilgrims. In 1928, two years before official Church recognition of the apparitions and of the cult of Our Lady of Fatima, the Archbishop of Evora, a large city in southern Portugal, decided to have a real church built at Fatima. The work went on for over twenty years and the new temple was solemnly consecrated by the Patriarch of Lisbon, Cardinal Manuel Ceijeira, on the 14th May 1953. The following year, Pope Pius XII raised the church to the level of basilica in his apostolic letter "Luce Suprema". The Basilica of Fatima, designed by Pardal Monteiro, is a modern construction, dominated by an imposing tower. The interior is quite simple, covered with a boxed vault, and the main altar is decorated with a painting which represents the scene of the apparitions and the personalities connected to the cult of Our Lady of Fatima -Bishop da Silva of Leiria, Popes Pius XII, John XXIII and Paul VI. The stained-glass windows tell the story of the message of Fatima and show scenes which illustrate the Loretan liturgies. The enormous tower, 65 metres high, dominates the facade of the church. The bell tower is the most striking element of the shrine and is surmounted by a crown and a cross which weighs seven tonnes. In a niche above the main entrance is a statue of Our Lady which was made by an American priest, Father Thomas McGlynn OP. In frónt of the church there is an immense open space enclosed on either side by two porticos under which are situated the Stations of the Cross in majolica. The open space is almost twice as big as that of St. Peter' s Square in Rome, and can hold around a million people. Nearby there are two other buildings, the Convent of Our Lady of Carmine and Our Lady of the Sorrows Hospital. In the hospital there is a chapel known as the Chapel of the Adoration of The Most Holy Sacrament, which is decorated with a painting by the Italian artist G. Lerario and also a stained-glass window representing the "Dance of the Sun". It should be pointed out that the Shrine of Fatima was built at Cova da Iria, that is to say on the slopes of the little hill where Lucia and her cousins grazed their flocks.

Today, Francisco and Jacinta would not recognize their childhood haunts. Since the beginning of the century, all that remains is the oak tree where the children were at the time of the visions, and the Chapel of the Apparations, constructed on the site of the tree at which Our Lady showed herself. The chapel, built according to the instructions given by Mary, is the most intimate and moving corner of the Shrine. It is home to the first statue of Our Lady of Fatima, that sculpted in 1929 by José Ferreira Thedim. In 1982 the chapel was refurbished and lost a little of its original simplicity. The square in front of the basilica is dominated by a monument to the Sacred Heart of Jesus, in the form of a column topped by a statue of Christ and an enormous cross raised on the occasion of the Holy Year in 1950. There are some other monuments on the square, like the statue of the Immaculate and statues of Pope Pius XII, Pope Paul VI and Bishop José da Silva. Not far from the basilica lies the Pastoral Centre inaugurated by Pope John Paul II, which is now the headquarters of the Blue Armada and also houses the offices of several religious orders. The village of Aljustrel is approximately two kilometres from the Shrine. The houses of Lucia, Jacinta and Francisco are now open for visits and some of the rooms are exactly as they were during the childhood of the young shepherds. Behind the house of the dos Santos family is the well where the

second vision of the Angel took place. Near Aljustrel are the other two sites, Valinhos (the fourth apparition of Mary on 19th August 1917) and Loca do Cabeço (the first and third apparitions of the Angel, 1916). A small chapel with a statue of Our Lady was built at Valinhos in 1956 and a monument was erected at Loca do Cabeço which shows the children kneeling at the feet of the Angel. Around these sites, the Via Dolorosa winds its path. Along the way, in the midst of the greenery, the oaks and olive trees, the fourteen white chapels of the Stations stand out. The Station representing the crucifixion is situated on the roof of the Chapel of St. Stephen. This Via Dolorosa was donated by Hungarian immigrants and for this reason it is also known as the Cardinal Mindszenty Stations or the Hungarian Cardinal's Stations. It should be mentioned here that this Hungarian cardinal made a pilgrimage to Fatima in 1972 and celebrated Holy Mass in the chapel dedicated to the patron saint of Hungary, St. Stephen. When visiting Fatima it is worthwhile going to see the parish church where the children were baptized. Also of note is the cemetery where the mortal remains of Francisco and Jacinta lay until their removal to the basilica, where their parents, and those of Lucia, were also buried.

View of Fatima.

The shrine at Fatima.
The interior of the basilica.

The belltower of the basilica.

The Chapel of the Apparitions.

High altar painting.

The windows of the basilica.

Jacinta's tomb.

Francisco's tomb.

Pope John Paul II at Fatima (13th May 1982).

Lucia 's house.

The well near Lucia's house.
The house of the Marto family.

Francisco's room.
Jacinta's room.

Valinhos: The Chapel of the Apparitions. Below - Loca de Cabeço: Site of the apparition of the Angel.

The parish church.

The baptismal font.

The Stations of the Cross at Fatima.

Calvary.

Calvary.

Pilgrimage of Pope John Paul II to Fatima 12-13th May 1982

Act of Entrustment and Consecration to the Virgin, in Fatima

1. "We seek refuge under Your protection, Holy Mother of God"! Repeating the words of this antiphon, with which the Church of Christ has prayed for centuries, I have come here, t() this place which You, Mother, have chosen and loved in a special way.

I am here, united with all the pastors of the Church by that special bond, through which we constitute one body and one college, as Christ wished the Apostles to be united in Peter.

In the bond of such unity, I speak the words of this Act, in which I wish to embody

Pope John Paul II in the Chapel of the Apparitions.

once more, the hopes and fears of the Church in this modern world.

Forty years ago, and again ten years later, your servant Pope Pius XII, with the painful experiences of the human family before his eyes, entrusted and consecrated the whole world to your Immaculate Heart, especially the Peoples who were in a special way the object of your love and your thoughts. This world of men and nations I too have before my eyes today, as I wish to renew the act and consecration made by my Predecessor in the Chair of Peter - this world which is drawing near to the close of the second millenium, this contemporary world, this modern world of ours!

Mindful of the words of Our Lord: "Go ... and make disciples of all nations ... And remember, I am with you always, to the end of the age", the Church renewed its awareness of its mission in this world with the Second Vatican Council. And therefore, Mother of men and nations, You who "know all their suffering and all their hopes", You who maternally feel all the battles between good and evil, between light and darkness, which rouse the modern world, hear our cry which, moved by the Holy Spirit, we direct to Your Heart, and embrace this human world of ours in the love of a Mother and Servant, this

The statue of Our Lady of Fatima.

world which, being full of anxieties for the earthly and eternal destiny of man and nations, we entrust and consecrate to You.

"We seek refuge under your protection, Holy Mother of God"! Do not scorn our prayers, we, who are being tested!

Do not despise; Accept our humble trust in you and our plea for protection!

2. "For God so loved the world that he gave his only Son, so that everyone who believes in him may not perish but may have eternal life".

It was with just this love that the Son of God could consecrate himself saying: "For their sakes I consecrate myself, so that they too may be consecrated in the truth".

By force of this consecration the disciples of every age are called on to dedicate themselves to the salvation of the world, to add to the suffering Christ has made for the benefit of his Body which is the Church.

Before You, Mother of Christ, and in the presence of your Immaculate Heart, I wish today, together with the whole Church, to join our Redeemer in his consecration of the world and of men. Only in his Divine Heart lies the power to obtain pardon and receive expiation.

May the power of this consecration last for all time; may it embrace all men, all peoples and all nations. May it overcome all evil, which the spirit of darkness is capable of rekindling in the hearts of men and in history, and which has, in fact, been reawakened in our time.

The Church, mystical Body of Christ, joins in our Redeemer's consecration, through the service of the successor to Peter.

How deeply we feel the need for the consecration of mankind and the world, this modem world of ours, in union with Christ himself! Christ's redeeming works must be shared by the world through the Church. How much hurt is felt when in the Church and in each of us, there is something which opposes sanctity and this consecration! How much it hurts to know that the call for repentance, conversion, and prayer, has not met with due observance!

How much it hurts to know that many participate so coldly in the Redeeming works of Christ! That our bodies manifest so insufficiently "that which Christ's suffering lacks".

Therefore, may the souls of all those who obey the call of eternal Love be blessed! Blessed be all those who, day after day, with inexhaustable generosity, hear your call, Mother, to do as Christ your Son tells us and to give the Church and this world serene evidence of a life inspired by the Gospel.

Above all, may You, the Handmaid of Our Lord, who in the fullest possible way obeys the Divine call, be blessed!

May You be praised, You who are completely at one with the redeeming consecration of Your Son! Mother of the Church! Enlighten the people of God on the ways of faith, of hope and of charity! Help us to live with the whole truth of Christ's cosecration of the entire human family of this modern world.

3. We entrust to You, Mother, the world and all men and nations; we alo entrust to You that same consecration of the world, that you may hold it in Your Maternal Heart.

O, Immaculate Heart! Help us to overcome the evil which can so easily take root in the hearts of today's man and which in its immeasur-

Pope John Paul II with some children from Fatima.

able effects, already threatens our modernity and seems to be closing off the paths towards the future! Save us from famine and war! Save us from nuclear war, from incalculable selfdestruction, from all manner of war! Save us from sins against human life, even in its earliest stages! Save us from hatred and the degradation of the dignity of God's children! Save us from all manner of social, national and international injustice! Save us from the ease with which we tread upon God's commandments.

Save us, save us from the sins which we commit against the Holy Spirit! Mother of God, hear our cry, filled with the suffering of all men! Filled with the suffering of our whole society!

Reveal to us once more through the ages, the infinite power of Merciful Love! May it stop all avil! May it trasform men's consciences! May the light of Hope be revealed in Your Immaculate Heart!

John Paul II in front of the statue of Our Lady of Fatima.

Pope's Act of Entrustment to the Mother of God (13th May 1991)

1. **"Holy Mother of the Redeemer**, Gate of heaven, Star of the Sea, help your people who want to rise again."

Once again we turn to you, *Mother of Christ and of the Church*, gathered at your feet in Cova da Iria, to thank you for what you have done in these difficult years for the Church, for each of us, and for all humanity.

2. **"Monstra te esse Matrem!"** How many times we have invoked you! And today we are here to thank you because you always listened to us.

You showed yourself a mother:

Mother of the Church, a missionary on this earth's roads towards the awaited third Christian millennium;

Mother of all people by your constant protection which sheltered us from disaster and irreparable destruction, and promoted progress; and modern social conquests.

Mother of the Nations by the unexpected changes which restored confidence to peoples who were oppressed and humiliated for so long;

Mother of life, by the many signs with which you have accompanied us, defending us from evil and the power of death; *My Mother* for ever, and especially on 13th May 1981, when I felt your helpful presence at my side;

Mother of every person who fights for life which does not

die. Mother of the humanity redeemed by the blood of Christ.

Mother of perfect love; of hope and peace, Holy Mother of the Redeemer.

3. "**Monstra te esse Matrem!**" Yes, continue to show yourself a mother to everyone because the world needs you.

The new conditions of peoples and the Church are still precarious and unstable.

There is the danger of replacing Marxism with another form of atheism: which, praising freedom, tends to destroy the roots of human and Christian morality.

Mother of hope, walk with us! Walk with the men and women along this last furrow of the 20th century with the people of every race and culture of every age and condition.

Walk with the people towards solidarity and love, walk with our young people, the craftsmen of future days of peace.

There is need for you in the nations which recently acquired room for freedom and are now committed to building their future.

There is need for you in Europe which from East to West cannot reclaim its true identity without discovering its common Christian roots.

There is need for you in the world to resolve the many violent conflicts which still threaten it.

4. "**Monstra te esse Matrem!**" Show yourself the *Mother of the poor* of those who are dying of hunger and illness, of

those who are suffering from torture and other abuses of power, of those who cannot find a job, a home or refuge; of those who are oppressed and exploited, of those who are without hope, or who in vain seek quiet far from God. Help us to defend life, a reflection of divine life, help us to defend it always from its dawn to its natural end.

Show yourself a *Mother of unity and peace*.

Stop violence and injustice everywhere, help harnony and unity grow in families and respect and understanding among peoples.

May peace, true peace, reign on earth!

Mary, give the world Christ, our peace. May peoples no dig anew the pits of hatred and revenge; may the world not yield to the desire for a false well-being which harm the dignity of the person and endangers forever the resources of creation.

Show yourself the *Mother of hope*!

Watch over the the road which still awaits us.

Watch over the people and the new situations of peoples still menaced by the threat of war.

Watch over the leaders of the nations and those who influence the fate of humanity.

Watch over the Church which is always threatened by the spirit of the world.

Especially watch over the coming Special Assembly of the Synod or Bishops, an important phase in the path of the new evangelization of Europe.

Watch over my Petrine ministry in the service of the Gospel and the human person towards the new goals of the Church's missionary activity.

Totus tuus!

5. In collegial unity with the pastors, in communion with the entire People of God spread to the four corners of the earth, today I *renew* the filial entrustment of the human race *to you*.

With *confidence we entrust eve ry one to you.*

With you we want to follow Christ, Redeemer of mankind.

May weariness not overburden us, nor hard work slow us down; may difficulties not extinguish our courage nor sadness the joy of our heart.

Mary, Mother or the Redeemer, continue to show yourself *Mother of all*, watch over our path.

May we joyfully see your Son in heaven.

Amen!

John Paul II *with* **Sister Lucia**.

The significance of Fatima

Il y a plaisir d'être dans un vaisseau battu de l'orage, lorsqu'on est assuré qu'il ne périra point.
Les tribulations qui travaillent l'Église sont de cette nature.

Blaise Pascal, Pensées.

In order to fully understand the significance of Fatima, two elements need to be taken into consideration: Our Lady's message and the testimony of the children who were privileged to see Mary.

The message of Fatima is a chapter in the history of salvation, and is a sign given by God to His Church. It can be summarized in the evangelical obligations of prayer and repentance. Christ, on many occasions, invites man to pray as an intimate dialogue with God: "So I tell you, whatever you ask for in prayer, believe that you have received it, and it will be yours" (Mk 11:24). We can

John Paul II at Jacinta's tomb.

find an exhortation to pray in the apparitions of the Angel and Our Lady. What would our faith mean if we were unable to speak to the Lord! Even in the first vision, the Angel taught the following prayer: "0 God, I believe in You, I adore You, I have hope in You and I love You! I ask You to pardon those who do not adore You, love You or have hope in You". He adds: "Pray this way. The Hearts of Jesus and Mary hear the voice of your supplication". In the second vision the Angel requests the children to recite this prayer to the Most Holy Trinity, to expiate the sins of humanity. Our Lady instead asks the children to say the rosary daily. In this way she tells us that to recite the Hail Mary, the Our Father and the Gloria, as well as to meditate on the mysteries of the Rosary, are the most effective prayers within the reach of most. Mary repeats her son's warning: "Be alert at all times, praying that you may have the strength to escape all these things that will take place, and to stand before the Son of Man" (Lk 21:36). The message of Fatima is also a call for penance. The story of mankind is one and the same time the story of infidelity to the Creator, and the succession of man's conversions in a continuous search for God. There cannot be real conversion without repentance and suffering. In these hedonistic times no-

body wishes to suffer, and medicine offers all the necessary means to suppress pain and at times even carnes out attacks on life itself, in the *form* of euthanasia. For most men, there are no positive elements to suffering. The dominant culture of modern times is quick to accuse a man who does penance, who voluntarily makes sacrifices, of being "mediaeval" or masochistic. Too often we listen to others, forgetting the words of Jesus: "...unless you repent, you will all perish as they did" (Lk 13:3). Even the Fatima visions began with a piece of advice from the Angel: "Offer to God every sacrifice you can, as an act of contrition for sins against Him, and to beg for the conversion *of* sinners". Mary, instead, asks the children in her first apparition: "Do you want to offer yourselves to God and to bear all the suffering He will send you, as an act of contrition for the sins of those who have wronged Him and to petition Him for the conversion of sinners?". On hearing the affirmative reply of the children, Mary revealed their destiny to them: "Then you will suffer greatly, but the grace of God will be your comfort". Our Lady was to repeat this request to do penance in later visions: "Sacrifice yourselves for all sinners and repeat many times, particularly when you make some sacrifice, 'Jesus, it is for your love, *for* the conversion of sinners and to expiate sins committed against the Immaculate Heart of Mary!' "(third vision), "Pray, pray a lot. Make sacrifices for the sake *of* sinners, as many souls go to hell because there is no-one to make sacrifices and pray for them" (fourth vision), they must mend their ways and beg forgiveness of their sins" (sixth vision).

Even from the lives of the children themselves can a message for mankind be seen. Francisco and Jacinta reached the peak of Christian sanctity. Their lives arouse admiration and respect in our hearts and at the same time teach humility to the "worthless servants" that we are. At Fatima, as at Lourdes, Our Lady confides her message to poor shepherd children with no deep religious education. In this way God carries out His evangelical promises: "Blessed are the poor in spirit, for theirs is the kingdom of heaven. Blessed are the meek for they will inherit the earth. ... Blessed are the pure in heart, for they will see God" (Mt 5:3-6) and "Truly I tell you, whoever does not receive the kingdom of God as a little child will never enter it" (Mk 10:15). At the beginning of the 20th century, God reminds man of the eternal truth contained in His Word, using the most innocent and apparently incompetent people. Purity of heart, though, counts for much more than intellectual quality for God. How can we forget Jesus' words to the "intellectuals" of his time: "Woe to you lawyers! For you have taken away the key of knowledge; you did not enter yourselves, and you hindered those who were entering" (Lk 11:52).

This is what the Bishop of Leiria writes about the message *of* Fatima on the fiftieth anniversary of the visions (13th May 1917-1967): "Its message contains a doctrinal content which is so vast that it can certainly be stated that no fundamental themes of our Christian faith have been ommitted. To God the Creator and Provider who cares for even the smallest of His creatures; these creatures who, at the highest level, as angels, place themselves at the service of man; the whole of nature which manifests itself as the work of God in portentous signs, to show divine Providence and Omnipotence; the sins which destroy the order of all beings and find their home in the power of Evil and in its ultimate result - hell; the Redemption of Christ through forgiveness and repentance; our solidarity with the mystical body of Christ, in expiation to the Hearts of Jesus and Mary; the sacraments of life, particularly that at the centre -the Eucharist; filial devotion to the Pope and

he Church; that most inti-
nate and fecund qualities of
a state of grace - when the
Most Holy Trinity dwells in
he souls of the just, the
growth of this life through the
undamental Christian
virtues of faith, hope and
charity, in the wonderful
prayers of the Angel; through
he moral virtue of prayer, repentance and alms-giving;
hrough a life of piety, fed
with solid, traditional devo-
ion, as so beloved by the
Church - the Rosary and devotion to Our Lady of the
Sorrows, of Carmine, of the
Holy Family, of the Immaculate Heart of Mary, with the
fundamental practice of expiation and consecration...;
with this eschatalogical vision of the future, Fatima
looks at the Church in one of
its essential dimensions and,
at the same time, places it in
its context of the historical
march of time ... could more
be asked of Fatima? Yet,
without doubt, none of this is
put forward by the message
as being something "new".
Everything is presented with
the simplicity of a catechism
lesson, which the best of
teachers, the Most Holy
Mary, gives her chosen

pupils, the little shepherd children". Fatima also teaches optimism. The unpredictable and very often dramatic lot of this world and of each single inhabitant, often allows people to become pessimistic, provoking the conviction that evil is omnipotent and weakening our faith. To Mankind, lost and afraid in the 20th century, Mary transmits her message of optimism: "My Immaculate Heart will triumph in the end!". If we really live our pilgrimage to Fatima, we will return home having rediscovered the meaning of prayer and suffering and with the edifying conviction that Christ is Lord of the world and of all time.

Around Fatima

Fatima is situated in the centre of the Estremadura, an historical region of the Iberian peninsula, which extends from Lisbon and Setubal to Leiria. It runs along the Atlantic coast and reaches inland as far as the valley of the Tagus and is characteristically flat with some hilly areas. The highest point of the Estremadura, Mount Serra de Montejunto, reaches 666 metres. The hills are covered with several different types of oak (quercetum) and are cultivated with olive trees, vines and cereal crops.

The caves of the Estremadura

In the central limestone mass of the Estremadura, a National Park has been created called Serra de Aire and Serra dos Candeeiros. The numerous caves are the park's largest tourist attraction as they are open to visitors. The most important of these caves are the "de São Memede" or "da Moeda" caves and particularly the "Mira de Aira" or "dos Moinhos Velhos" caves. The "da Moeda" caves were discovered in 1971 and are relatively small, being about 350m long. They are divided into nine beautiful sections each formed from rocks of differing colours. The Shepherd's Room is -particularly beautiful. The "Mira de Aira" caves were discovered in 1947 and are made up of a complex series of tunnels and rooms which reach a length of 4 kin and include a stream which forms pools along the way. One of the rooms reaches imposing dimensions - 110m high and 50m wide. There is a stairway of 583 steps to descend to the lowest level. Also of great interest are the "Alvados" caves, discovered in 1964. These have a large central area and 10 side rooms, each with its own pool. The stalactites and stalagmites are so big that they form great colums. Here, the many different colours of the rocks are brought out by excellent illuminations. Finally, there are the caves of St. Anthony, which were discovered in 1955. They

are made up of 3 rooms, the largest of which is 43m high, and an underground lake. The unique colours of the limestone formations, together with a large number of stalagmites create something of a fairy-tale atmosphere.

Batalha

In the town of Batalha, in the district of Leiria, lies the Abbey of Our Lady of Victory (Mosteiro de Santa Maria da Vitoria). It is a classic example of Gothic art, and is not only one of the most important national monuments in Portugal, but is also renowned as one of the most interesting monastic complexes, architecturally speaking, in the whole of Europe. Its construction is linked to the foundation of the Aviz dynasty of Portugal. In 1383, after the death of the king, Dom Fernando I, his daughter Beatriz was the only person in line to the throne of Portugal. Beatriz was married to King Juan I of Castile and according to mediaeval custom, Portugal should have become united with Castile. The Portuguese, however, did not wish to give up their independence and one military leader, the Master of Aviz, drew up his army to fight the Spanish. Before the decisive battle, the Master of Aviz made a vow to Our Lady promising to build a monastery in her honour should the battle go his way. On the 14th August 1385, the battle took place near the village of Aljubarrota. Despite the superior numbers of the Castilian army, the Portuguese had the best of the fighting thanks to their courage and determination. With this victory, Portugal was able to retain its independence and found itself with a new king - the Master of Aviz, who took the name of Dom João I. He became the founder of a new royal dynasty which reigned successively for two centuries, a time which included the period of the great geographical discoveries by Portuguese navigators. The construction of the monastery began three years after the battle, at a site about 15 km from Aljubarrota and was named in honour of the great event - Batalha (Battle). The initial work was carried out under the Portuguese architect Afonso Domingues from 1388 to 1402, but it was an English builder, Master Huguet, who completed the project in the years between 1402 and 1438. The most important part of the abbey is the church which is 80rn long and 22m wide. The church faces west and the choir east and there are three naves, a transept and choir with four chapels at the sides. The entrance to the church is through a deep arid richly decorated portal. Resting on shelves in the obliquely-cut walls of the doorway are finely-sculpted canopies with statues which show biblical figures. The tympanum is covered with a frieze of sculpted images from the lives of Christ, the Apostles and, above these stands the crowned Mary. Above the portal, there is a splendid Flamboyant window. To the sides there are two other smaller windows which correspond to the lateral naves. On the right, we can see the walls of the Founder's Chapel (capela do Fundador) which was specially built for Dom João I by Master

Batalha: Side entrance to the church.

Batalha: Detail of the portal.

Batalha: Abbey of Santa Maria da Vitoria.

Huguet. It is square-shaped (20m on each side), but the chapel contained within is octagonal and is topped by an ogival vault. The whole is decorated with stone stars. In the centre of the chapel lies the royal tomb with a statue representing Joa-o I (d. 1433) and his wife, Philipa of Lancaster (d. 1416). The royal couple are shown holding hands tenderly, and over their heads rise mediaeval canopies. Beside the central sarcophagus, lie the tombs of other members of the royal family of Aviz, Fernando the Saint, João, Henry the Navigator and Pedro. One tomb missing is that of the eldest son, Dom Duarte, which lies behind the choir of the church. Much later, the tombs of some more recent royal descendants were added, those of Dom Afonso V, Dom João II and Prince Afonso. The dimensions of the church are imposing. The vault, which rests on eight pairs of pilasters, reaches 32m in height. The interior of the church is bare, the only decoration being the 16th century stained-glass windows. The contemporary choir window is particularly valuable. Adjacent to the north nave are the abbey's cloisters which are known as the Royal Cloisters (claustro Real). Their architect, Afonso Domingues, designed a rectangular courtyard of 50m by SSm, surrounded by wide-arched Gothic porticoes. Later, stone Manueline tracery was added, characterized by arabesques, plant-shapes,

armillary spheres and crosses of the Order of Christ - a real lacework, sculpted in stone From the cloisters we pass into the Chapter House (casa do Capitulu). It is a masterpiece built by Master Huguet, who managed to cover a large room of 1 9m square with a vault which has no central pillar. Today, the Chapter House contains the Tomb of the Unknown Soldier. On the other side of the cloisters, there is the refectory beside which is a lavabo containing a large bath mounted on two smaller ones. There is also a second cloister in the abbey, named after Afonso V (claustro de Afonso V) which seems to have been built in two stages - the first, Gothic and the second, Renaissance Behind the choir are the breathtaking Unfinished Chapels (capelas Imperfeitas) so called because they were never finished or roofed. The king, Dom Duarte required a new sepulchral chapel for himself and his successors and asked Master Huguet to do the job in 1438. The work later passed into the hands of Mateus Fernandes who built one of the most beautiful, but unfortunately incomplete, structures in Manueline style ever. I is octagonal, has seven chapels and a monumental portal which leads to the vestibule and contains the tombs of King Eduardo and his wife. In the adjoining chapels the tombs of other historical Portuguese figures can be admired. The monumental portal, which is a re

Batalha: The Royal Cloisters.

Batalha: The Unfinished Chapels.

Batalha: The Royal Cloisters with fountain.

fined example of Manueline architecture, deserves special attention. It is composed of tens of small columns, which have been finely sculpted with geometric and floral motifs. The columns finish in trilobate arches, covered with the same decoration. The mausoleum was never roofed; the architects only erected the imposing pilasters which jut out above the chapels' vaults. Although fragmentary, the whole complex is nonetheless most evocative.

Alcobaça
Abbey of Santa Maria

In the midst of the Estremaduran hills, between the Alcoa and Baça rivers, lies Portugal's most famous monastery - the Abbey of Santa Maria of Alcobaça (mosteiro de Santa Maria). Its history begins in the 12th century when, in 1147, Dom Afonso Henriques, the first King of Portugal, conquered the area around Lisbon and the Estremadura. Four years later, having received the consent of St. Bernard, he invited some monks of the Cistercian Order into the new kingdom. He granted them a vast but marshy area, of uncultivatable land between Leiria and Obidos. The monks built a monastery at Alcobaça, which was destined to have an important role for centuries as it became a centre of religious and scientific life. It was particularly well-known for its theological school and its patronship of the arts - the monks were protectors of architects, sculptors and painters. The Benedictine tradition included the copying of books, and the abbey library became one of the biggest in Portugal. From the 13th century onwards, the monastery also played the role of public school and pharmacy. The Cistercians also had an effect on the economic situation of the surrounding area. The Rules of St. Bernard required the monks to do physical labour and so they cleared forests, reclaimed marshland and tilled the earth. A wilderness was thus transformed into vineyards, orchards and cornfields. They even introduced the cultivation of cotton which supplied the local workshops with raw materials for clothmaking. The monks also contributed to the local ceramics and metalworking industries. The heart of the abbey is the Church of Santa Maria. The original church was built in 1178 but was destroyed by the Arabs as early as 1190. Then, at the beginning of the 13th century, reconstruction commenced and building came to an end during the reign of Dom Dinis (1279-1325). A monastery was built near the church in the style of Clairvaux, the cradle of the Cistercian Order. Even today, the beauty of this monastery can be admired and it is without doubt the most important Cistercian building in Portugal. The noble, austere interior of the church is of truly imposing dimensions, 20m high, 23m wide and 106m long. The central nave is divided from the rest of the church

Alcobaça: General view.
Alcobaça: Facade of the church.

by twelve columns. Two narrower naves of the same height run parallel. All three naves lead to the transept, behind which is the choir with a large ambulacro. The chapels lie radially around the choir. In the transept two royal sarcophagi are displayed - those of Dom Pedro I (d.1367) and of Inés de Castro (d.1355). The tomb of Dom Pedro I is a large, stone coffin resting on six lions. The upper part holds a statue of the dead king flanked by six angels; at his feet there are two dogs sculpted by an unknown artist. The sides are completely covered with beautiful bas-relief work, telling the life story of St. Bartholemew, the king's patron saint. On the other side of the transept is the tomb of Inés de Castro[*]. A statue of this lady supported by six angels lie& on the sarcophagus. The sides show sculpted scenes from the life of Christ and on the ends

we find scenes representing the Day of Judgement and the Crucifixion. These sculptures from the royal tombs at Alcobaça are among the most important in Portuguese art.

As has already been said, the monastery in Alcobaça resembles its model, the Abbey of Clairvaux. Beside the church are the square cloisters off which there is a large refectory, the kitchens, the Chapter House, a dormitory and the workshops where, amongst other things, the copying of books was undertaken. The "Silent Cloisters", or the "Cloisters of Dom Dinis" as they are also known, are the largest of their kind in Portugal. They were built to two different plans, the first being from the 14th century while the second dates from the 16th century and is a fine example of a typically Portuguese style which developed in the late Middle

Alcobaça: The "azulejos" of the Royal Chamber.

Ages, known as "Manueline". The name derives from a Portuguese king, Dom Manuel I, who reigned from 1495 to 1521. The Chapter House is situated on the eastern side of the cloisters. The interior is square and covered with a vault which rests on four pillars. Nearby, a stairway leads to the dormitory, a large room with two rows of columns surmounted by decorated capitals. Under the dormitory is an area where the monks once carried on manual tasks and which also served as a scriptorium where books were copied. The large refectory gives onto the northern side of the cloisters. It measures 30m by 23m and is divided into three naves by two rows of columns. In the monastery's golden era, the refectory was used by several hundred monks and still today we can see the lectern used for readings of the sacred scriptures at mealtimes. Beside the refectory are the kitchens with their huge chimneys and the baths of the lavabo which received their water from the River Alcoa. It should be added that the kitchen was rebuilt in 1752 and the majolica tiles on the walls date from this period. Also from the 18th century is the Kings' Chamber, the entrance to which is off the western wing of the cloisters. This name derives from the collection of statues of the kings of Portugal which are kept here, together with a group of terracotta figures and a statue of Our Lady. The walls are covered with tiles known as "azulejos". These "azulejos", used as wall and floor tiles, have played such an important part in Portuguese art and architecture that the

*Alcobaça: **Tomb of Dom Pedro**.*

Alcobaça: The Silent Cloisters.

history of their use should be explained. "Azulejos", glazed ceramic tiles , were known and produced in Spain (Alhambra, Seville) as far back as the 14th century. Previously they had been used in Morocco and in fact their name comes from the Arabic "az-zulay", meaning "small piece of terracotta". At first, from the 15th- 16th centuries, they were decorated with mostly geometrical Arabic designs. From the 17th century on, more figurative designs appeared and the height of their use came with the period of the reign of Dom João V (1706-1750). The walls of churches and palaces built at that time are covered with wonderful blue and white painted tiles showing scenes both sacred and profane. Returning to the church of Santa Maria, it should be added that the facade and the whole western wing of the abbey were renovated in the 17th and 18th centuries in the Baroque style. The only medi-aeval remains are a bare portal with a large window overhead. The facade is embellished with Baroque statues of Our Lady, St. Bernard and four personifications of the Virtues, while two bell-towers have also been added at the sides.

Nazaré

On the Atlantic cost of the Estremadura, on a bay surrounded by two high, limestone headlands is the town of Nazaré, an old fishing village and today a popular tourist resort. Nazaré consists of the three districts of Praia, Pederneira and Sítio. The old harbour lies in Praia, where in the past there were only fish warehouses and boatyards. Today, thanks to an increase in construction which has not always respected the environment, the whole amphitheatre of the bay is filled with hotels, and the promerrade with bathing establishments. It is famous for its fish and you can still see the traditional brightly-painted fishing boats. You may even be lucky enough to catch a glimpse of someone wearing the traditional costume of Nazaré; for the men, checked shirts and black woollen hat with pompon - for the women, black skirts with petticoats, sometimes richly embroidered. On the southern headland is the oldest part of Nazaré - the district of Pederneira. In olden times it was a small fishing village. The houses of the fishermen are grouped around the central square which is also home to the church, the Igreja Matriz. A second church, the Igreja da Misericordia, dating from the 16th century is further up the promontory and from the square in front you can get marvellous views of the whole bay and the harbour. On the other side of the bay, on the highest promontory of the entire Portuguese coast, 110m high, is the district of Sftio with its world-famous sanctuary of Our Lady of Nazaré (Nossa Senhora de Nazaré). A statue of Our Lady venerated in all Portugal is kept in the sanctuary. There is an ancient legend which says that in the 4th century, a monk called Ciriaco brought a small statue of Our Lady to Bethlehem where he presented it to St. Girolamus. Later, St. Girola- mus donated it to St. Augustine who sent it to the Monastery of Merida in Spain. During the Saracen invasions, King Rodriguez and a monk, Brother Germanus, hid the effigy of Our Lady in a cave on the Atlantic coast in a place called Sítio. The statue was discovered by chance in 1179 by some shepherds. A few years later a nobleman by the name of Dom Fuas Roupinho was hunting deer in the area of Sítio. While pursuing one, the hunter suddenly found himself about to go over a precipice, his horse already with one hoof over the edge, when suddenly Our Lady appeared to him. The man began to beseech her for help and was miraculously saved. Dom Fuas Raupinho had a chapel

Nazaré: General view.

built and placed the statue of the Virgin therein. Later, a church was built around the chapel and Sftio became a place of pilgrimage. Among the countless who haye prayed to Our Lady of Nazaré, are Vasco da Gama, who visited the church before undertaking his voyage to India, and St. Francis Saverius, the greatest missionary of Asia.

Church of Our Lady of Nazaré.

Nazaré:*The old chapel.*
Nazaré: *Fishmonger.*

Nazaré: View of the town.

A fisherman in Nazaré.

Drying the fish.

Nazaré: Fishing boats.

Index

PHOTOGRAPHS: ARCHIVIO PLURIGRAF
BRUNA POLIMENI: COVER - PAGES. 3 - 10 - 56 - 58 - 59 - 60
- 61 - 63 BELOW - 64 - 65 - 66 - 67 - 80- 81 - 83 - 85 - 87 -
88 - 89 - 90 - 91 - 92 - 93 - 94 ABOVE - 95